Connecting with the Land:
Nature Relationships in Multiple Dimensions

Second Edition

Authored by Adam M. Davis, Ph.D.

ISBN-13: 979-8712652754
ISBN-10: 8712652754

This book was originally published in 2013, with color photographs and a different cover. This second edition, which became available in 2023, features "gray scale" versions of originally published color photographs and multiple additional nature connection techniques.

DEDICATION

This book was written in service to land and people. It is dedicated to *Carya ovata*, *Ursus americanus*, the Susquehanna River, the Port Deposit Gneiss, soils, the Salem Limestone, Half Moon Mountain, creeks and rivers, the Billy Goat Trail, bedrock, Lake Erie, the barrens, barred owls, skunks, Hoosier National Forest, bald eagles, the Scarce-o-fat Ridge Trail, vultures, Catoctin Mountain, Hickory Nose, robins, Mugwort Grove, trees, Connecting with the Land Workshop Series celebrants and supporters, land stewards, the Raquette River, ancestors of techniques, the Appalachian Mountains, Amethyst Brook, my friends, my teachers and mentors, Ben Nevis, wildflowers, the Potomac River, my blood relatives (living and dead), and other entities and energies of the sacred Earth.

ACKNOWLEDGEMENTS

Artwork was done by Adam M. Davis, except Figure 2.3 (by Evans and Perlman) and Figure 22.1 (by Kasper Kalavaris). Photographs were taken by Adam M. Davis, except the one in Figure 7.2 (by Mark Davis) and the author photograph (by Mischa Kern). All contributions are greatly appreciated.

The nature connection techniques of the book have come to Adam Davis through a life-long personal dialogue with the land, decades of naturalist training from diverse sources, workshop and ceremony facilitation since 1998, training in diverse traditions of spiritual practice, councils of all beings, overlapping threads of shamanic journeys, and other conduits. He was given techniques by numerous mentors and teachers over the years: earth and environmental scientists, Naturalists, shamans, pipe carriers, Yogis, herbalists, Qi Gong masters, Druids, environmental activists, his first scoutmaster, his students, and others. Adam is grateful for these gifts and honored to be called to pass along the wisdom.

Special thanks to Arlene Davis, Becca Allen, Mark Davis, Jon Peters, and Sulis Sunrise Sophia for reviewing manuscripts of this work before the publication of the first edition.

TABLE OF CONTENTS

CHAPTER 1. Introduction, purpose, and use of the book.

Have you ever felt a deep sense of calm or awe when out in natural surroundings? Have you been inspired by a breathtaking view from a mountaintop? Are you overcome by a sense of wonder as you witness water flowing along a creek bed? Do you experience joy when seeing young foxes emerge from their den? If you have experienced emotional and inspirational transformations in situations like these, you have likely benefited from a heightened sense of connectedness with the land. Would you like to expand upon these types of experiences? Would you like to become more aware or intentional about them? If so, this book may be supportive of the next steps in your journey.

Through "Connecting with the Land: Nature Relationships in Multiple Dimensions", I aim to help you realize relationships that you have with many aspects of the land, find new ways to nourish your spirit, and receive guidance for living in greater harmony with nature. This book is designed to be a practical guide, providing tools and strategies for being intentional about nature experiences, for delving deeply into them, and for expanding the set of activities you can use to connect with nature. Many ways of connecting are covered: opening to inspirations from nature's beauty and diversity; strongly identifying with a particular animal, tree, or natural feature; investigating the power of place; reading omens from nature; meditative and shamanic techniques; and more. The methods I describe in this book have come to me through scholarship, mentorship, personal practice, classes, ceremonies, and sharing within "Connecting with the Land" workshops by people from diverse backgrounds. Many different disciplines and world views are represented in this work.

Through use of the techniques in the book, you can develop relationships with nature that nourish your spirit (your sacred essence). You can embrace nature as a significant part of your life and as a contributor to your wellbeing. In my personal spiritual practice, I draw from a repertoire of methods (a toolbox) that includes many of the techniques for connecting with nature that are discussed in this book. The following story provides a window into my practice and an example of intentionally connecting with nature:

> In the late afternoon of a mid-July day in a forest of western New York State, I decided to consult the local land, seeking guidance for the next phase of my life. I let my intuition guide me to a spot along the bank of a small creek in the woods. Sitting on the forest floor at this place, I observed the plants and soil, and I felt the air and diffuse sunlight on my cheeks. I let myself become aware of the sounds of the forest. A nearby patch of soil caught my attention, and I focused my awareness there – visualizing myself diving down into the soil, moving between the silt and bits of decayed leaves. Then I paid attention to an apple tree with three entwined trunks, leaning out over the small creek valley. I thought of an old Celtic meaning associated with the apple tree, shelter for deer, which helped me feel comfortable and safe in the presence of this particular tree. The entwined trunks inspired me to direct and integrate the trajectories of several energy currents in my life. Inspired and relaxed, I focused my eyes on one point in front of me, paid attention to my breathing, and allowed impressions to come into my mind from the landscape. As I was sitting, a

young robin landed in my lap after taking his first flight. I removed him from my lap and we stared at each other until he decided to hop off to the west. After sitting a while longer, I walked out of the small valley and was greeted by a woman. She welcomed me back from my journey with a hug and purified me with the smoke of burning white sage. Over the next several days, I allowed an interpretation of the robin omen to emerge. Scientific knowledge of robins was helpful in my search for meaning – the robin gets its food from the soil and returns to some areas in the spring season. Traditional spiritual meanings associated with the robin were also useful to ponder, especially that this bird marks a new direction. The fact that it was a bird learning to fly was inspiring to me. The young bird told me to move out of limbo (the nest) into a new phase of my life.

Several techniques present in this story are discussed in the following chapters. You can learn to use them as tools for connecting with nature.

Before delving into the toolbox, I provide philosophical context and tips for optimizing the effectiveness of the techniques covered later in the book. Chapter 2 discusses our connectedness with nature, and Chapter 3 indicates benefits that come from intentionally interacting and communicating with nature. Chapter 3 also covers broad underlying themes and fundamental practices that can help you get the most out of the specific techniques mentioned in other parts of the book.

If you are called to jump right in and add tools to your vibrant nature connection practice, feel free to skip over the introductory material. You can randomly open to a page and read about the method discussed there, or use the index of techniques in the back of the book to go directly to the one you want by using its "T" number. In the body of the book, the numbered techniques are typically followed by a "how to" paragraph that provides instructions to help you get started. Supplementary information is available from many of the references that are listed at the end of the book and cited (author, year) throughout. This book is a starting point as well as an ongoing source of fundamental ideas and techniques for the development of nature relationships. I invite you to pick and choose the methods that work best for you and to customize them to fit your circumstances, which includes working with them in a balanced, healthy, safe, and sustainable way. I encourage you to find your own style of exploring and communicating with nature and at the same time appreciate the ways of others. Join me in being as present in each moment as possible so that we can embrace opportunities to deepen our nature relationships.

Let us become aware of nature's complexity and infinite beauty. Let us dive into the water like a loon and also skim the surface like the swallows. Let us burrow in the soil as a woodchuck and fly high with the eagle. We can connect through science and environmental service as well as shamanic journeying. The sky is not the limit, and neither is the core of the Earth. Let us play, and let us work hard. We can explore our own integrity as we learn about nature. Let us dare to open our minds and our hearts. We can experience through all of our senses and through many ways of knowing. Let us love and feel part of the whole. We can both intellectually reason that we are part of the Earth and feel it in the core of our being. Feel the call of the wild beating in your heart.

CHAPTER 2. Everything is connected.

"We are part of the earth and it is part of us" Chief Seattle

Many different kinds of relationships among parts of ecosystems (natural systems of various sizes within the overall Earth System) have been described by scientists, including relationships between the non-living/environmental parts of ecosystems and the living parts. Figure 2.1 shows connections between soil, rock, water, sunshine, and plant communities that have been revealed to be part of ecosystems.

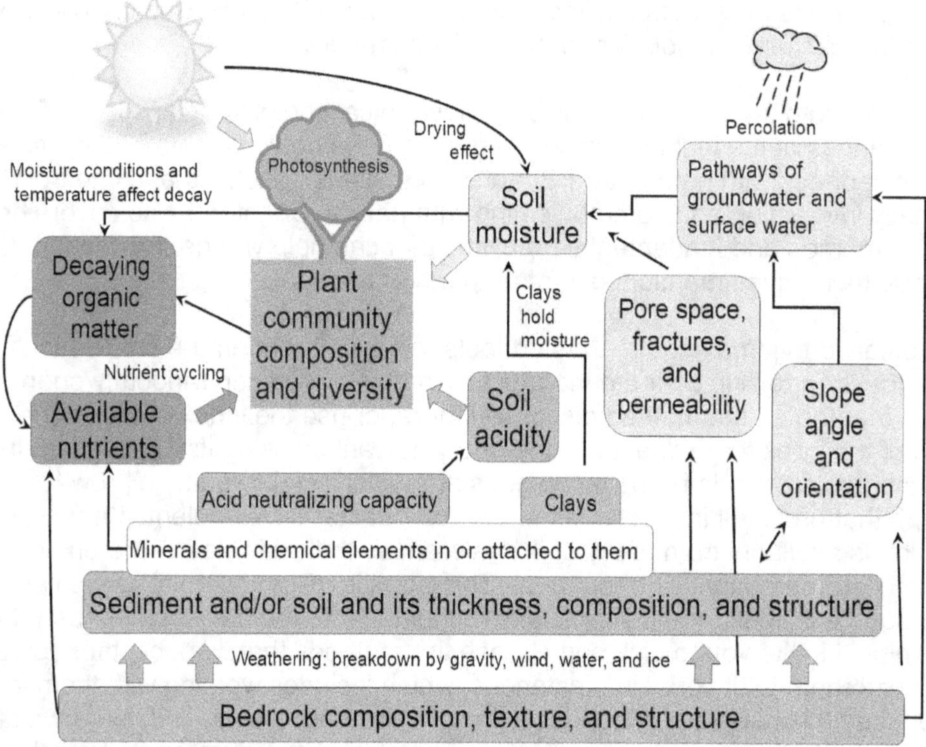

Figure 2.1. Conceptual model that focuses on the factors influencing plant community composition and diversity (Davis, 2011).

In ecosystems, living things can be related by competitive, cooperative, antagonistic (e.g., predator-prey), and other kinds of relationships. The relationships may be intentional or not. Species can influence one another through both direct connections and complex networks of cause and effect.

We humans are connected with the land, nature, our environment, other living things, and the Earth as a whole in many ways. Humans have a niche or role, often a dominant one, in ecosystems of which they are a part. Human activities affect the operation of the Earth as a whole. We are all part of the hydrologic cycle (the ways that water moves between different areas within the Earth System). We breathe the air, and we contribute gases to the atmosphere. We drink from rivers, lakes, and groundwater; our sewage ends up in rivers, lakes, and groundwater. The cotton in our commercially made clothing was grown in soil that was formed by the breakdown of rock, irrigated with waters pumped from the ground or diverted from rivers, harvested and processed with machines that burn fossil fuel extracted from the Earth, and made into clothing using electricity derived from a mix of natural resources. Plants that we eat get their sustenance from sunlight, nutrients in the soil, and groundwater (see Figure 2.1). So the food in our bellies contains the essence of the soil, water, and air of the farms where it was grown as well as human and natural resources used to harvest, process, and transport this life giving food to us. Our shelters and the way we keep warm also connect us with the planet. Both primitive and complex homes are built with Earth materials such as wood, quarried rock and minerals, metals, and petroleum based materials. And there are many more ways that we connect with aspects of the Earth, land, and nature. A general ecosystem model that includes food web relationships (relationships between types of living things based on "who eats who") and human activities is shown in Figure 2.2.

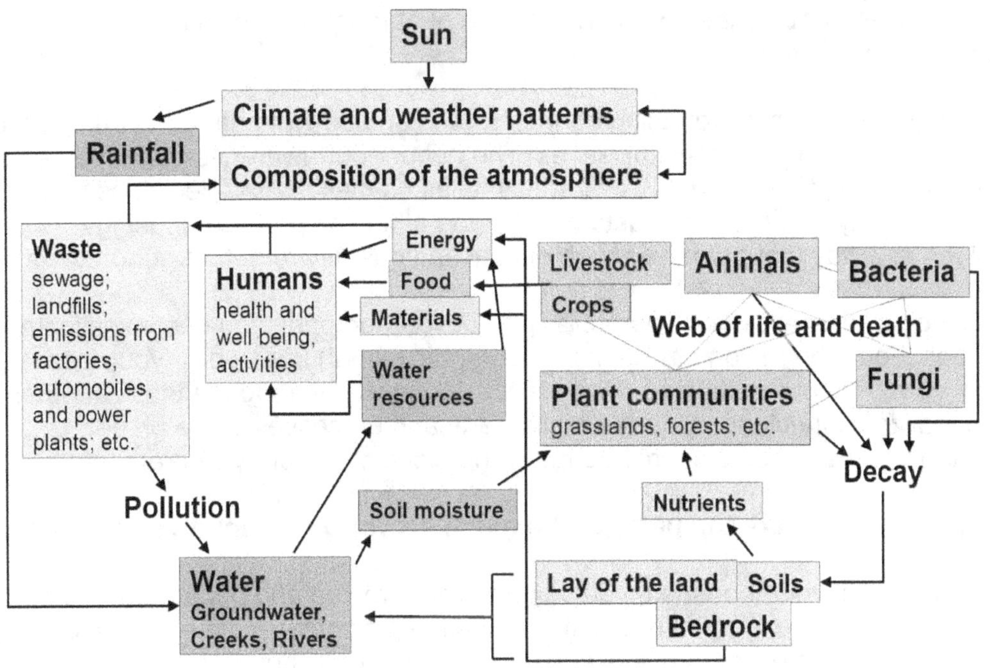

Figure 2.2. Generalized ecosystem diagram relating fundamental aspects of the Earth System, including human activities.

We can enhance our awareness of the connections within the Earth System that relate to our basic survival. We can then expand upon this basic nature awareness by learning what natural resources were the raw materials for our clothes, walls, computers, automobiles, telephones, and other aspects of our built environment. We can take it further by examining the many environmental consequences involved in resource extraction processes and in the transport of products to us. We can trace materials used in our houses and household items back to the forests that were logged, back to the landscapes that were altered by quarrying of the bedrock, and back to the wells that pump fluids out of the Earth.

Our lifestyles, actions, and decisions influence the workings of the ecosystems and indeed the whole Earth System of which we are a part. We influence current and future generations of the web of life. We have a quantifiable impact on natural resources and environment, an ecological footprint, which influences regions all over the globe. The first specifically labeled technique of the book (T2.1) involves the calculation of the impact of one human's choices on the planet's resources.

T2.1. Calculate your ecological footprint.
Examining your ecological footprint is a way of learning how everything, including your behavior, is connected. A generalized footprint can be calculated with computer software applications accessible online (one footprint calculator is provided by the Global Footprint Network at URL: https://www.footprintcalculator.org, as of 3/21/2023) and more detail can be achieved by looking at the footprint of each activity. Among other ways, your footprint could be expressed in amounts of resources used per unit time or as an estimate of number of Earth's required if everyone lived like you.

As we begin to see how everything connects, we can see that natural resources are at the root of many of our societal issues. The deeper our awareness, the greater our potential to change our impacts. Awareness helps us make better decisions and helps the society move toward sustainability (the ethic and practice of using resources in a way that preserves their quality and quantity for future generations).

To enhance awareness of one particular part of your footprint, you can investigate your "foodshed" [the region or regions (geographic extent) from which your food is hunted, gathered, and cultivated (Hahn, 2013)]. Knowing your foodshed is another way to realize connectedness to the many parts and processes of the planet (i.e., soils, farmers, resources that provide fuels and electricity, factory workers, etc.).

T2.2. Identify and mark the parts of the globe or world map involved in your foodshed.
To get a sense of your foodshed, you can ask your grocers and restaurant managers about the origin of the food. Although it is sometimes a complicated mystery to unravel, you may enjoy the process and discussions that spring from asking about the geographic origin of the food that you eat. Upon considering the paths traveled by the foods I consume, I have realized the magnitude of the planetary resources that I have used. Such use by everyone on the planet is not sustainable. This realization motivates me to remove certain foods from my diet so that I use fewer natural resources. As part of coordinated efforts to move toward sustainability, people have worked to reduce the size of their foodsheds (Nabhan, 2001). What foods can you eliminate from your diet to shrink your foodshed and reduce your environmental impact?

Humans, along with all life on the planet, are intimately linked to how water moves through various regions – collectively known as the hydrologic cycle (aka the water cycle) and shown in a general form in Figure 2.3.

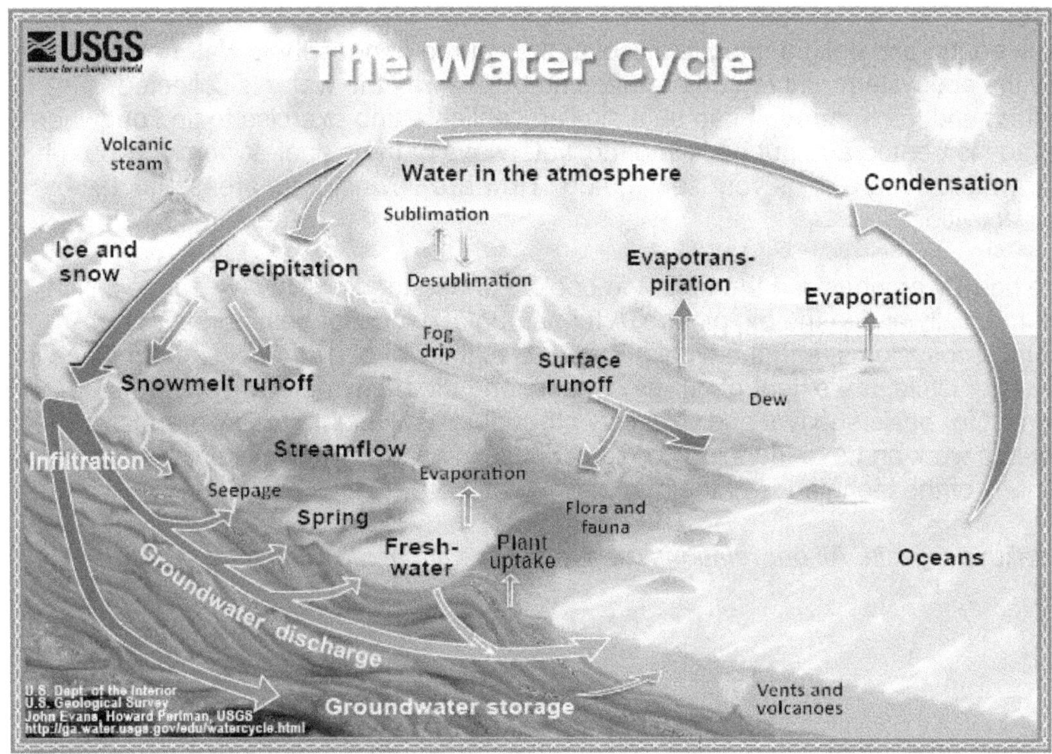

Figure 2.3. Generalized depiction of the hydrologic cycle (aka water cycle), which is the movement of water through the Earth System.

In many urban and suburban residential areas, rain that lands upon lawns travels into the ground, flows in the pore spaces between soil particles, and then flows out into a local creek (or ditch, brook, run, or other names for small streams). Or, if the rain falls on a road or parking lot, water could travel directly into the creek via storm drains. Once in a creek, water can flow downstream into a larger creek or river and then into progressively larger rivers. It may eventually make its way into a wetland, a pond, a lake, a human-made reservoir, or an ocean. The water can evaporate from these bodies of water and travel with air currents as water vapor. The water can condense in clouds and then precipitate as rain drops once again. The cycle varies from place to place, there are often multiple pathways within each local system, and all water bodies on the planet are connected when a long enough time period is considered.

Humans interact with many local and regional expressions of the water cycle. Through our interactions, we have impacts on the movements and chemistry of water. The cycling of water matters to us because our drinking water reservoirs and waters that nourish crops are part of the cycle, among other reasons. Pollution from household waste, pesticides and fertilizers applied to farm fields, and toxic releases from industrial activities all travel with the waters. Where do you get your water? What water bodies do you pollute through your actions?

T2.3. Find out where you get your water and where your household wastewater goes.
It can be fun and enlightening to discover the source of household water and to learn how the ecosystem and region are affected by the way the water is collected, treated, and transported. It can be a similarly enlightening exercise to find out where sewage is treated and put back into the waterways of the planet. Where do you get your water? Where does your sewage go? How are downstream areas affected by your activities?

One heavily emphasized theme in the book is understanding how we connect with nature locally and in the big picture. A fundamental aspect of being present with nature, ecosystems, and the whole Earth is a high level of awareness of our place in the water cycle, the extent of our foodsheds, and the many other ways that we connect for basic survival and to satisfy other desires. Heightened awareness of how systems work and experiencing connectedness in a variety of ways are key aspects of many of the techniques in the book.

"Mitakuye Oyasin. All our relations." *Lakota affirmation, blessing, and prayer*

CHAPTER 3. Sensing and developing spiritual connections with nature.

We are connected with nature in many ways. As beings of nature, all that we do is spiritual. A woman washing, kissing, and anointing feet is highly regarded by the divine (Luke 7:36-50), and passing a pipe and smoking is a spiritually nourishing act. When asked "What is the Buddha?" by a monk, Zen Master Ummon (Yunmen) replied "a dry shitstick", which was a stick used for stirring the excrement in a latrine (Wikipedia, 2013a). The realization that everything is spiritual is important for cultivating a spiritual awareness and a "plugged-in-ness", and has been equated with the idea of enlightenment. This book is based on the principle that the ethereal idea of enlightenment is contained within the practical actions of connecting with nature, Earth, and Universe.

"Washing dishes is like bathing a baby Buddha. The profane is the sacred. Everyday mind is Buddha's mind." Thich Nhat Hanh

Our daily actions, priorities, and lifestyles define our relationship with nature because we are an interconnected part of the system. Everything we do is a way of connecting with the land, both forging and reflecting our spiritual connection with nature. We can encourage an unconscious emptiness of spirit through the way we work with the land; or we can emphasize nourishment, purpose, and service.

If we are connected to the land in so many ways, our spirit is not separate from us, and/or we believe that everything we experience or do is spiritual, then why should we bother being intentional about spiritual connections with aspects of nature? What are the benefits of nature connection work? What techniques might we want to cultivate? Read on for a discussion of benefits and fundamentals here in this chapter. Later chapters offer specific ways of connecting that are listed in a technique index at the end of the book.

Benefits of developing relationships with the land

There are many reasons for being present and engaging with nature: improved health and quality of life, pursuit of knowledge, greater ability to make informed decisions, integration of ethics and religion, inspiration and spiritual nourishment, encouragement of a state of deep connection with nature, and others.

1. Personal health and well being

Walking, sitting, and being in natural or wilderness areas can have a calming effect as well as bring peace of mind. The stress and anxiety that can accumulate through daily activities may just melt away while sitting by a river and quieting the mind, or while hiking along a trail in the forest. Studies have shown that physiological changes occur as a result of spending time out in nature. Reduction of stress and depression, faster healing time, and less need for pain medication are all effects demonstrated by empirical research (Louv, 2012).

Many of us have special places that we go for recharge and renewal, favorite trails, and places we like to stop along the trail. I have a number of specific places that I go to recharge: places along slopes of mountains, individual trees and groves, places along various creeks and rivers, ridges and hollows, places rich in wildflowers, and stark landscapes scarred by human activity. I retreat to these personal spots to lay on the Earth Mother's placenta and receive her nourishment. Spending a little time sitting in these places renews my spirit. Immersion activities like sleeping under the stars or swimming provide stronger recharge and lasting transformation for me (see chapters 10 and 18 for further discussion of this effect). We may not be aware of all of the ways that a place can nourish us. Perhaps this is the spirit world, the divine, or the great mystery working with us.

Our physical health depends on natural resource quality. Clean air, clean water, and clean healthy soil for our crops all nourish us. When the land is healthy and when ecosystems are healthy, we can be healthy. We desire the resources that the Earth provides and we are at its mercy in this regard. We want relationships with nature that nourish us rather than harm us.

"Everybody needs beauty as well as bread, places to play in and pray in, where Nature may heal and cheer and give strength to body and soul alike." John Muir

2. Feeling the richness of community

Relationships with trees, animals, rivers, and mountains can nourish us socially in a way that expands our sense of community. Interacting with them can bring us joy similar to when we interact with a small happy child or people we love. We can experience many other types of emotions like we do while working within human communities. We may be uplifted and inspired by colors in the clouds at sunset or a chorus of tree frogs in the evening.

3. Drinking from the fountain of knowledge

Through a program of intentionally maintaining relationships with nature and employing the techniques of this book, we can cultivate an enhanced sense of our place in the Multiverse and of how the whole Earth System works. Working with diverse techniques can help us learn about our connections to specific parts of the Earth, cause and effect dynamics within ecosystems (at multiple scales), and consequences of our land use and lifestyle decisions.

People that have an insatiable curiosity for pursuing the "great mystery" of existence acquire knowledge and understanding while keeping alive the desire to learn more as well as the desire to look through new lenses. This tremendous drive to understand is an unquenchable thirst, because the mystery always remains. "The way that can be spoken of is not the true way" (Lao Tzu), and folks have a drive to find the true way. Many have philosophically explored the ineffability of existence. In the 1700s, Immanuel Kant advanced the idea that our knowledge, observations, and perceptions are based on and therefore limited by our experience of the world. He suggested that we do not observe and perceive the actual processes occurring on the planet or in the Universe. He encouraged the idea that our minds are key to what we experience and know (Lavine, 1984). Our senses have physical limitations in terms of the portion of the electromagnetic spectrum we can observe, the varieties of sounds we can hear, the reach of our touch, what we can smell, and other aspects of sensory experience. Various authors have summarized our extremely limited observational abilities [e.g., Descartes (2013)]. Basically, we have such a limited view that we cannot see what is happening. And yet, we have a rich history of learning about our world.

Past cultures accumulated and communicated complex and intricate knowledge of Earth workings. Archaeological evidence reveals that the Druids, Mayans, mound building North American tribes, and other cultures possessed insightful wisdom about the natural world. Roman and Greek scholars investigated and communicated their Earth wisdom through the written word. Pliny's "Natural History" includes many metaphysical (deeper meanings or implications of the physical) and medicinal qualities of plants, minerals, and rocks that are reused by modern authors (Pliny, 77-150/1956; Cunningham, 1988; Kozminsky, 1988). Pliny showed his passion for understanding the Earth as he died by inhalation of poisonous gases while studying the eruption of Mt. Vesuvius (Wikipedia, 2013b). The seventeenth, eighteenth, and nineteenth centuries (CE) brought tremendous advances in understanding of the natural world by early pioneers of the natural sciences (e.g., Thomas Jefferson, James Hutton, Charles Lyell, and Charles Darwin) (Livingstone, 1992; Levin, 2006). Some of these Naturalists empirically observed nature as a way of learning about God's creation. Chapter 5 gives us a sense of modern day opportunities that we have to satisfy our desire for nature knowledge.

"Curiosity killed the cat" American folk saying

4. Learning to make different decisions

Many of us care about nature, about our health, and about the health of children. We may live with the intention of respecting other inhabitants and aspects of the Earth. We care, but we can still make poor decisions if we remain ignorant or have poor information. We need to know which of our actions add to our planetary resource footprint and which reduce it. A thorough understanding of natural forces and our energy exchanges with the land can inform lifestyle, land use, environmental, and resource management decisions that will slow the degradation of our environment.

We can cultivate awareness of our connections to other parts of the Earth, and in the process become more aware of the consequences of our consumer choices and the consequences of supporting particular land uses or construction projects. We begin to see how our decisions affect quality of life for future generations. With a heightened sense of cause and effect, we can decide to optimize ecosystem health, which can help us optimize our own health and health of the children. We can be frugal with natural resources, learn how to live sustainability, make smart land use decisions, and support sound environmental policy.

5. Ethics, cultural traditions, religion

"Just trying to do the right thing" American folk saying

"Let the trees be consulted before you take any action" John Wright

"Healing ourselves and working to resolve the contradictions in the human-Earth ecology is the same work" Elizabeth Roberts and Elias Amidon

When we talk about minimizing impacts on the environment or minimizing our footprint, we are also talking about treating other beings, the planetary system, and ourselves with respect. Our cultural, ethical, and religious drives are wrapped up in how we connect with the land. So doing it in an ethical and compassionate way can give us the satisfaction of doing the right thing. Our emotions of love, empathy, and compassion are engaged. Our principles of respect and justice as well as our theological and philosophical concepts of divinity, separateness, and oneness are woven into our relationships with the land. Nature ethics and heartfelt emotions are expressed in poetry, prose, prayers, and song.

"Oh, Great Spirit, I pray for the environment. I pray for its cleansing and the renewal of our Mother Earth." Ed McGAA, Eagle Man

Some of us engage nature directly in our religious ceremonies, and others aspire to do so. For many of us, nature honoring traditions are part of our cultural heritage even as degradation of nature is also part of our heritage.

"When the planet herself sings to us in our dreams, will we be able to wake ourselves, and act?" Gary Lawless

6. Inspiration and nourishment of spirit

"… a leaf of grass is no less than the journey-work of the stars" Walt Whitman

Many have waxed romantically about nature's beauty. Breath-taking views may awe us, babbling brooks may fill us with wonder, and we may befriend the faces we see in trees or clouds. When I take time to be fully present and observe nature, I am impressed by its diversity and complexity. After some nature time, I find that I am able to restore my creative juices – maybe the Earth Mother gives me some of her milk. Empirical research corroborates the inspiration effect: University of Kansas researchers found a 50% boost in creativity after spending time immersed in nature, and University of Michigan workers found a 20% increase in memory and attention span after just one hour in nature (Louv, 2012).

Nature can enliven and inspire us in many ways. A profound, sustained inspiration as well as feelings of happiness and wholeness are possible through a vibrant nature connection. We nourish our spirit through the way that we work with nature and the land. We may rejoice and give thanks for the opportunity of life and desire to make the most of it. We may be inspired to support efforts to conserve or preserve nature's beauty.

"May your trails be crooked, winding, lonesome, dangerous, leading to the most amazing view." Edward Abbey

7. Deep nature connection

We may never understand the great mystery of the Multiverse and our existence, but we can try to cultivate a holistic understanding of the Earth System, perhaps related to what Arnie Naess called a "deep ecology" (Foundation For Deep Ecology, 2012). We can derive contentedness from opening to rich, vibrant, multivalent (through many states of being) connections with nature. We can feel a sense of belonging. We can achieve a greater awareness of our many nature connections.

Our connection deepens through studying and working with nature: regularly engaging the mental, spiritual, and physical aspects of our being. We learn to see from different perspectives, and we allow energies to pervade and transform us. This deepening can be spotty, cyclic, or a progression. A progression of deepening is illustrated by a Nanao Sakaki poem: see mountain → climb mountain → climb self → there is no mountain or self.

Sprinkled throughout the book, quotes from insightful authors convey some of the less tangible desires for connection, reasons for striving to connect, and results of deep connection. They get us in touch with some of the instinctual, intuitive, and heartfelt reasons that people strive for deep nature connection. By relating on a spiritual level, we can cultivate a deep awareness of nature and its workings. Through deep connections, we can develop a greater understanding of the consequences of land use decisions and personal consumption choices as well as a greater understanding of how to respect the land and nature.

Connected
Conscious
We watch with awe the flight of the hummingbird
Maybe we feel a twitch of joy
Aware of the connections
Intentionality
Knowledge and awareness could allow us to deliver respect
Respect for other beings in the system
Respect for future generations
We may intend to be respectful
But we lack awareness of our connections
Or purposely avoid thinking about the impacts of our actions
We don't know where the dominos fall when we impact one
We don't know the stakes or consequences of our choices
So we fail to deliver respect
We feel the pain of the clearcut

And the shame of our role in it
A raw nerve is exposed
The Lorax has no trees
The Ents are going to war
Warriors are chained in solidarity in the path of bulldozers
Mountains are leveled
A root comes out of an acorn and penetrates the thin mountain soil
Adam Davis 6/4/2013

Deep connectedness leads to awareness of environmental impacts and affects the inspiration we derive from visiting places in nature. It can lead to responsible intentionality regarding our actions within the planetary system. We begin to connect intentionally with greater wisdom. We can live sustainably: in a way that uses natural resources at a level that can be maintained without depleting or degrading them for future generations of living beings. Let us get to the business of changing our lives, to the practice of connecting with the land.

Cultivating spiritual relationships with the land

Although words cannot relate the depth and possibility of nature connection, the text of this book opens the door to the possibilities by presenting methods for intentionally seeking and developing a deep, profound sense of connectedness with natural places and nature in general. It describes techniques for deeply connecting or "plugging-in" to nature in a way that alters the practitioner's physical, emotional, conceptual, philosophical, and spiritual being. Put another way, the book's goal is cultivation of relationships with the land that engage the spirit more deeply than does the typical mode of operating employed by main stream society. I invite you to develop your nature connections by opening your senses in new ways that provide a multidimensional understanding of the diversity and beauty of various places on the planet. Doing this work leads to extra nourishment, inspiration, love, and a sense of belonging to the Earth.

The techniques in this book work better and can add to a cumulative effect when they are part of a continual practice of connecting that is integrated into our lifestyles and is as regular as possible. Such a regular practice focused on connecting with nature helps us deepen and transform with the techniques in this book. They evolve with us as we make them our own.

Before making room in your lifestyle for one of these methods/techniques, I suggest considering whether it is ecologically sound (whether it makes good sense given your situation). It may be helpful to ask yourself questions. Does that technique feel right for me at this time? Does the frequency of the planned use of the method fit my circumstances? Is my plan for incorporating it sustainable? Incorporation and use of the techniques in this book should be done in a healthy, safe way. Consulting advisors, guides, and intuition may help ensure the highest quality of spiritual nourishment possible.

Aspects of my practice include dialogue with aspects of nature, meditating in specific places in the landscape, observing and listening to nature, tracking changes to places through the year, wandering and exploring new lands, intuitively stumbling upon interesting energy patterns, sleeping out, working with fire, seeking omens, and offering praise and service to nature entities and energies. This regular practice keeps me sane in this world, helps me be more aware of nature, and allows me to relate to the land on many levels.

A regular practice that combines many of the elements of the book supports becoming part of a culture of nature literacy. Together we can promote a culture that considers nature and natural energies in decision making, such as has been done by some tribal cultures. We can consult nature before making zoning decisions and before breaking ground on projects.

As part of my consulting practice, I have the privilege of helping people communicate with their land before deciding to make land use changes such as cutting down trees or otherwise clearing existing vegetation, landscaping, or building on the land. For example, I helped a woman investigate an area that included her ancestral property and an adjacent wildlife preserve. The following account of the experience illustrates the use of methods discussed in later chapters and shows some of the potential richness of relationships with the land.

> We walked the land, across ridges and stream valleys, along the boundary of a wetland, and through old fields and forests. We sensed linear energy patterns in the landscape related to ridges deposited by past glacial activity and sensed differences in the energy of an upland area characterized by thin soil above granitoid bedrock where glacial influence was less conspicuous. The linear ridges shaped energy conduits through the landscape, while the round hill underlain by granitoid bedrock had a cold, stark power spot at its summit with an ancient natural order in the forests on its slopes. We felt out a sheltered cove area in the wildlife preserve by listening, singing to the trees, and doing the Tsalagi Dance of Life. These activities helped us tune in to the energies present, and it became obvious that this was a place where people have naturally gathered for many generations. We also walked in circles in an old field area, sat in meditation, and journeyed – carried by a drum beat. I surveyed the horizon and opened myself to spirit energies of the land. Two faces came into my mind as I journeyed (possibly past inhabitants), and I got the feeling that this location was the site of ritual work in the past. My client and I looked to the future as well. The message we received was that several places in the landscape were ideal for future gatherings as long as the footprint is minimal, and the natural order is respected and preserved. I found it to be very rewarding to do this work with my client on her land. I loved that we fused a dialogue with the land with a dialogue with each other. We supported each other in intuitively moving with the energies and beings of the land. We deepened our understanding of the place by connecting with heart, mind, and spirit.

It is a joy for me to see people communicating and working with their land in order to make decisions that are fair to all inhabitants as well as the whole system. It is also rewarding to see folks engage with nature when they are considering making a land purchase.

General themes and basis of the techniques

A number of the book's concepts, ideas, and strategies relate to a few basic philosophical themes such as ineffability, the existence of many ways of knowing, and non-duality. In addition, many of the specific techniques described in the book are supported by some fundamental spiritual activities such as visualization, meditation, and communication.

Great mystery

The ineffability of the cosmos, existence, Earth, and nature can provide a sense of mystique and instill wonder in us. It fuels our curiosity and challenges our mental and philosophical faculties. We can struggle with or embrace the mystery. We seek names and concepts to describe the essence of our world: the causal nexus, the Earth System, living Earth (Lovelock, 1979), dynamic Earth and Universe, and others. Naming and conceptualization efforts remind us that we don't know.

"Nothing is as it seems, nor is it otherwise" Buddhist saying

Perspective change

In a journey during a sweat lodge ceremony, in which I was an ant crawling through the Earth, I received a message: shifting ever so slightly one way or another can provide an entirely different worldview (i.e., different outlook, dimensions of experience, set of emotions, collection of thoughts, set of inspirations, and more). A number of effective land connection techniques encourage us to shift how we sense nature and in the process incline us toward exploring from many different angles.

An ethic of an open mind and the cultivation of mental and philosophical dexterity are useful for enacting perspective changes. Also helpful is making a habit of consciously choosing to explore new ideas and new operating paradigms from which to view entities, energies, situations, and events. There are specific techniques that facilitate perspective changes and that help us establish a regular practice of enacting these changes of perspective. One method involves zooming out the frame of reference in an abstract way (e.g., imagining moving up or out to look at the big picture of the landscape). Other, concrete physical techniques are also useful for shifting between frames of reference and operating assumptions.

T3.1. Change speed of movement.
Slowing down your walking pace, possibly in response to some feeling of a change in the landscape or some "call" to do so, is an excellent way to shift perspectives. I like to employ this technique when hiking. While walking along a ridge in North Carolina, I realized that the trees were ethereal beings in an enchanted forest, so I slowed down to commune with the energies of the place. While walking the ridgetop of Mt. Holyoke in Massachusetts, an intentional slow down allowed me to scope plants and feel the mountain plant communities in a rich way. When I listened to my gut, I walked slower and the resulting perspective shift helped me become more

present with and connected to these places.

Transcending and/or abandoning our assumptions can be enlightening. Our cultural and economic backgrounds shape our vision and thought, and folks with different backgrounds can help us see the world from different views. As one example, homeless folks in the USA can remind us of the layers of material concerns that cloud our vision. The weather is not a distraction or secondary concern for the homeless – they experience it differently than those who live and work in climate controlled buildings.

Communicating with atypical words, language, or symbols is an excellent way to mark the sacred. It is a way to put yourself in a different mindset than normal, because you have to use your brain differently to work with the special symbols or language. Similarly, employing new or rarely used techniques can make you take a perspective different than you normally do. In the late 1990s, I was sitting in the living room of two of my mentors, and we were talking about the use of shamanic and ritual techniques for exploring energies and consciousness. At some point in the conversation, the mentors realized that I was not experienced with the use of postures in journeying. In response to this realization, one of them got out a book called "Ecstatic Body Postures" (Gore, 1995) and showed me the frog posture (squatting with tongue out). I still use this posture today when I feel like I need a perspective shift and/or want to let my full body be involved in shaping my state of consciousness. In August of 2013, another discussion with the same two mentors led to another teaching moment. This time, the other one taught me about connecting with specific aspects of nature using hand postures. I was inspired to intuit a custom posture for working with air currents along the Potomac River.

Incorporating regular perspective shifts, multiple ways of knowing, and viewing natural phenomena through multiple lenses into the spiritual practice can lead to reaping benefits such as personal growth and robust land connections.

Many ways of knowing

Related to the idea of multiple perspectives is the idea that there are many ways to learn and many ways to explore the great mystery. Science, faith, contemplation, meditation, art, language, and hidden mysteries are all ways of knowing.

Different conceptual frameworks for and approaches to learning about the Earth as a whole include global circulation models, the Gaia hypothesis – Earth as a living organism (Lovelock, 1979), geochemical cycling, weather pattern – ocean current – landmass linkages, studying the movements of the continents and evolution of the Earth's Crust, Earth Mother reverence/piety/religion/faith, elemental chanting, studying the evolution of life, and making an Earth Mother figure that shows the whole system (Zell, 1998).

Combinations of techniques are tremendously valuable for connecting with the land. One could combine multiple methods within one general way of knowing, such as the use of multiple working hypotheses for scientific inquiry (Chamberlin, 1965), and combinations can be made across traditions (e.g., the journey of a shaman combined with data collection and analysis of a scientist). Druidic traditions combine scholarship, research, field work, offerings, prayers, magic [according to Aleister Crowley "Magick is the Art and Science of causing changes to occur in conformity with Will" (Bonewits, 1971)], ritual, bardic expression, and artwork to explore nature connections. Figure 3.1 depicts many ways to connect.

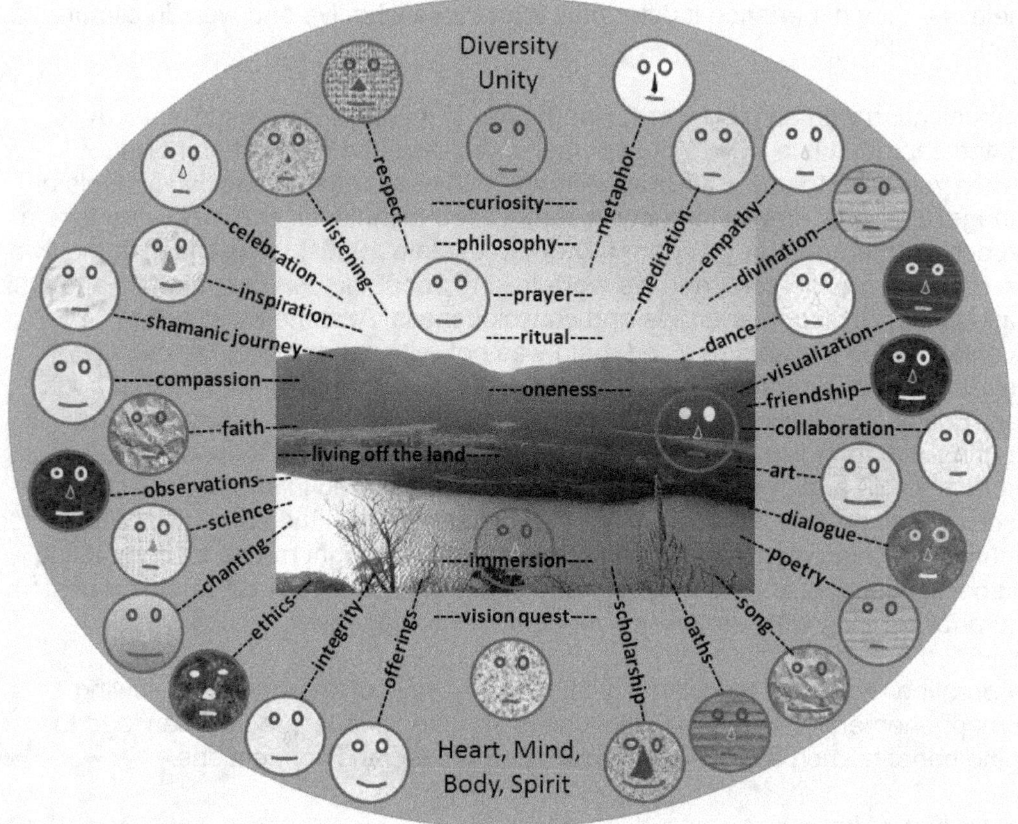

Figure 3.1. Illustration of many ways to connect with nature. We work with the land using a variety of states of consciousness and frames of reference. Many methods are available.

And all ways to connect can be worked with as one. We are the World Tree.

Focus and repetition

Even as there is value in seeing things from many angles and through many cultural lenses, focusing on one technique is also very important. In order to internalize techniques in this book, it is critical to practice them regularly. Doing one technique every day for years makes it your own, and still it changes through time. You and the technique coevolve.

Preparation

As with any vocation, a regimen of mental, physical, and spiritual exercises promotes success. "Sharpen the saw", "be prepared", and "work on the tradecraft" all apply. Cultivating a nature-educated mindset as well as physical health can be useful preparation for connecting with nature in multivalent ways. Meditation and other aspects of regular spiritual practice (conducted outdoors and/or indoors) help maintain readiness, ability to plug in, and heightened awareness of diverse happenings of the moment. Preparedness facilitates appreciation of natural diversity as well as deepening into the awe of a moment while immersed in nature.

The way that we connect is related to our health, emotional state, and state of mind. It can be very helpful to intentionally clear our minds and cleanse our bodies before and during the use of this book's methods. For some of the techniques, it will be useful to quiet the mind or let the analytical mind take a vacation. Smudging (purification with smoke from burning mugwort, sage, tobacco, or other substance) can bring the mind to the here and now. A regular meditative practice also helps.

Smudging, sprinkling with salt water, and vinegar sponge baths as well as a healthy diet can help cleanse the body. Eating healthy also enhances energy levels and consistency, so it is worthwhile to navigate available nutritional information and apply intuition toward finding an optimal nutrition philosophy and practice. A diet of mostly protein and vegetables keeps me cleaner, more aware, and more able to focus than a diet rich in carbohydrates. Another key to health is ensuring that healing gets done as needed. Fixing everything from tight muscles, to rotten teeth, to a foggy mind helps us connect more deeply. Exercise is also good preparation, as it keeps the brain supplied with oxygen. Sleep is important for ensuring mental alertness, although occasionally sleep deprivation provides a useful perspective shift. Drinking healthy amounts of water helps circulation and washes away toxins. Coming from a place of clarity, purity, health, and in touch with core values makes deep spiritual connection with nature much easier.

"Come from a place of fullness" Shannon Doran

T3.2. Be present.
Focusing on the breathing and then allowing the sights and sounds of a place to emerge can be a good way to become connected to the present moment. We can let go of obsessions of the analytical mind, and leave behind past obsessions, future trips, and other cognitive noise. We can honor the "monkey brain" and let it take a temporary vacation so that we can deepen our connection with the land. Techniques described in the coming chapters can help us commune and merge with nature as well as provide nourishment and inspiration in our daily lives.

Meditation techniques are useful as fundamental skills to be built upon for specific applications. Mindfulness, zazen, transcendental meditation, Qi Gong, Yoga, and other practices can be helpful. Postures and movements associated with meditative practices can raise awareness and enhance ability to plug in.

Visualization is another basic tool. Visualization can be done by picturing imagery in the mind's eye or allowing imagery to appear on the inside of our foreheads. It can be applied in many ways such as exploring surroundings on an imaginary journey through a landscape, or visualizing a journey into a tree and then imagining what it is like to be the tree looking out at the world. This Basic Visualization Technique (BVT) helps with the use of methods introduced in later chapters.

"All senses" approach

We benefit from optimizing our awareness of the information coming to us through our senses (tactile, olfactory, taste, auditory, visual, and more). We can work on broadening our senses in order to pick up more channels with our antennae, see multiple wavelengths, and more. Additional information can come into our psyches with physical sensations [known as clairsentience (Rosetree, 1996)]. Methods of this book, especially when used in a regular spiritual practice, get us in the habit of using all of our senses, which leads to greater awareness of many aspects of nature on many levels. Greater awareness of connectivity, including cause and effect in specific cases, can help us be more intentional and responsible regarding our energy exchanges with the land. Enhanced awareness enables nourishment of sacred core, essence, and spirit.

Sensing energy

Energy is defined scientifically as the ability of a system to do work on another system (Aguado and Burt, 2010). Each entity in the Earth System has its own energy state and potential (e.g., when you are tired you may say you have "low energy"). An entity's energy signature can be glimpsed through its state of vibration, through its aura [see Rosetree (1996) for more on auras], and otherwise. Energy signature relates to essence and spirit. And an entity, such as you or I, is also generating or part of specific energies or energy flows. Individual energies include the Earth's magnetic field, solar radiation, heat given off by your body, and gravitational pulls of Earth and Moon. There are many unique energies in the Earth System, and some of them affect us each moment. Energy changes or transferences (energy flows) that are associated with Earth System processes can be noticeable (e.g., wind in the hair). Feeling the Sun's warmth, seeing auras, and being affected by the Moon phase are all ways that our bodies sense energies. Each place has a unique set of energies and energy movements, and we can enhance our awareness of them and learn to be intentional about interacting with them. Many of the methods in this book involve engaging with the overall energy or individual energies of the land.

Deepening, plugging in, getting to oneness

Present, aware, and prepared, we can now deepen into our practice. We can now experience and work with the Earth in ways that are beyond our dreams.

Journey of the spirit	...	Carried by the winds
Journey of the spirit	...	We can go higher
Journey of the spirit	...	Tumbling down the stream bed
Journey of the spirit	...	We can flow with the energy
Journey of the spirit	...	Burrowing in the soil
Journey of the spirit	...	We can go deeper

Many tools and techniques used in the spiritual practice of major religions and by individual enlightened souls can be used to deepen relationships with nature.

T3.3. Learn oneness through faith.
Believing with your soul in oneness with the Earth and in your place as part of Earth can shape your connections and feelings of connectedness. While an intellectual understanding of connectedness provides a richness to our existence, our energies and spirits are enriched and stimulated to new levels if we believe in oneness through faith or religious conviction. Although it is difficult to describe how to create this conviction, I feel it resonate in me when I invoke aspects of nature in prayer or ritual, especially when I weave my essence into the invocation. Here is an example invocation of oneness:

> The waters that flow through the Earth, in creeks, and in rivers are my blood.
> The soil and rock are my flesh and bone.
> The wind and essence of air, they are my breath.
> I am a branch that connects to the World Tree. I am the root and the crown. I am the fire inside the Earth and inside the Sun.

Say these words out loud seven times, and note how it feels. Non-separateness is a tenet of Zen Buddhism, and Zen centers and retreats are useful for encouraging the belief of oneness. Reasoning the way to oneness can be a start.

"Your mind is always with the things you observe. So you see, this mind is at the same time everything." Shunryu Suzuki

T3.4. Attain through non-attainment. Flip the shamanic switch. Beginner's mind.
Deepening connection, plugging in, and being one with nature can be similar to the transformation required to begin a shamanic journey. Some shamanic practitioners use tunnel and tree constructs as pathways for journeys. Drums, rattles, and medicines can help journeyers set the brain waves, shift consciousness, and transform their beings (Harner, 1990). Some New Age folks (people who are part of the "New Age" wellness movement) use guided visualizations and carefully crafted music. I rise up and walk across the clouds, or sometimes along a ridge. Sometimes I take a path in the woods, or other times I am soaring above the landscape. This shamanic transformation may include "flipping a switch" in consciousness or energy to allow the journey to happen. This shift and other energetic transformations can allow deeper communing with energies of place. Flipping the switch is achieved by not flipping the switch, by allowing the journey to happen, letting the drum beat carry the mind's eye, and/or attaining through non-attainment. In shamanic practice, the allowing aspects of journeying can be combined with well crafted questions, intentions, and guidance from spirit allies.

Zen Buddhist practice helps cultivate a state of mind that is effectively a blank slate and ready to grow or journey. This is not a mind that thinks it knows things or that is burdened by models or constructs of knowledge. We want what Suzuki (1970) calls "beginner's mind", defined by Suzuki with the phrase "in the beginner's mind there are many possibilities, but in the expert's mind there are few". Beginner's mind can help with flipping the switch, and/or beginner's mind is the flipped switch.

T3.5. Spend time to deepen.
The states and experiences of deep connection (realizing the connection in an integrated, full body way) and oneness can defy description, and achieving these states may not require the use of predetermined techniques. But, the techniques in this book can help you let go of limitations and allow the energies of the land to work with you. Results of regular deepening work over time include deepening processes becoming habit and the ability to change levels of connectedness at will. Regular practice can help you cultivate deep levels of awareness, realize rich relationships, set you free of limitations, and have wise dealings with nature.

Importance of place

There are special places we can go: places along the trail, places to go to recharge, places to go for inspiration, and other places. Maybe we don't know all of why we stop and linger there at first. We may not be sure of all of the ways that these places nourish us, as they are part of the great mystery. However, if we open up and pay attention, a place can show us how to interact with it. Spontaneous work driven by cues from the land can be more rewarding than following through with a pre-planned set of techniques. Information from the land helps us go deeper.

T3.6. Explore new places.
Exploring new places can be a very enlivening activity. I feel activated mentally and spiritually when I explore a place for the first time. I especially like to move through the place in an intuitive, free-flowing way using ad hoc combinations of techniques to work with its unique energies. Chapter 9 discusses the sacredness of places, and Chapter 23 explores the art of combining multiple methods.

Integrity, honor, and respect

We can work with the land as our authentic selves:
- Honest with self – not in denial.
- Self aware and aware of surroundings.
- Knowing the difference between core values and emotional reactions.
- Treating the web of life with respect.
- Coming into a place of connection with benevolence, a good heart, and meaning well.

Can we choose to relate in ways that nourish the spiritual awareness, feelings, and energy exchange we have with the land? YES! Can we do this and be in integrity with ourselves and our tribe? YES!

Just do the work

While work with big picture concepts can enhance understanding of processes and themes involved in connecting with nature as well as support analysis of cause and effect, the specific techniques of the book work well when they are the sole focus of your energy and when you are not attached to results. It is not necessary to engage the analytical mind, because energy moves whether you perceive it or not. Find time in your schedule to be outdoors and make spiritual nature connections.

CHAPTER 4. Observing nature.

Getting out to natural areas and sensing what happens there is of prime importance in developing relationships with the land.

T4.1. Observe one place.

Sit and observe a place within a forest, park, or other natural area. Scope the diversity. You can get a glimpse of nature's infinite complexity through sitting for 30 minutes to an hour in one place. Just sit and allow yourself to notice your surroundings. You could write observations and impressions in a journal or field notebook. The notes may help you further investigate what you saw, along with the help of Naturalists and other references. You can figure out how the system works in this particular place.

The following is taken from a journal entry that I wrote while making observations from a dock and boardwalk located in a wetland at the end of Fitzgerald Lake (located in the state of Massachusetts, USA) in early October 2012:

> Insects are speaking to me today in this place – I have a stink bug sitting next to me on the bench, and various types of dragonflies are flying around. Bees and wasps are also buzzing around. A water strider is in the water next to me. Birds are calling, chirping, and flying in the sky above and in the forest that surrounds this wetland. Asters are flowering a few paces away, and a *Polygonum* species blooms next to me. The water is clear, a breeze is blowing, and sticks and leaves litter the bottom of the small open water area next to the dock. The twigs and leaves are atop, below, and mixed with fine sand and mud, and the mix is different each place I look. Tiny muscovite flakes in the sand reflect sunlight that has penetrated the water. I could delve more deeply into the composition of the mud, look for seeds or pollen, and identify the species to which the twigs and leaves belong. The cattails are in the act of dispersing their seeds, some of which float in the water while others are carried past me by the wind. The cattails' leaves bend and dance as the wind blows. Sedges and grasses grow in clumps along the dock. Maples, alders, pines, birches, and oaks of the nearby forest edge sway in the breeze. Chatter of insects can be heard in the background. Crows caw. While writing the journal entry, a blue sky with a few clouds has been replaced by a ceiling of gray stratocumulus clouds. Ducks quack and fly close to the lake in the distance. I hear the building rustle of the forest as the wind comes from a distance and draws near. In the 45 minutes that I have been sitting here, I have heard at least 8 different bird species at a slow time of day for birds. A frog talks near the dock. As I leave along a boardwalk, a grasshopper is jumping in front of me, I pass a 1/3 green and 2/3 black frog, and a bumble bee visits an *Aster*. I pass alder, dogwood, elder, *Viburnum*, and multiflora rose shrubs/small trees. Closer to the ground, I see multiple fern species, grasses, beggar's ticks, a more vine-like *Polygonum* species, jewelweed, a *Rubus* species, and the "lady's thumb" *Polygonum*. I walk by a place where a small stream flows under the boardwalk on its way out into the wetland. There are areas of gravel deposition, areas of sand deposition, and areas of mud deposition along the bottom of the half meter wide stream channel. Fallen leaves litter the boardwalk as I am now back under the forest canopy.

Figure 4.1. Fitzgerald Lake and surrounding wetlands and forests.

Each locale on the planet has a unique beauty and sacredness. The bedrock, landforms, soils, plant communities, animals, water pathways, climate, weather, and human influences all vary from place to place. Figure 4.2 shows some of the diverse beauty of North American landscapes.

Figure 4.2. Four different landscapes providing an inkling of the Earth's diversity: a) Black Hills, SD, b) Brattleboro, VT, c) Cranberry Lake, NY, d) Grand Canyon, AZ.

One type of natural feature that has similarities from place to place (e.g., a creek) can have other characteristics that differ substantially geographically. Figure 4.3 illustrates differences in the rock type diversity of stream gravel by comparing two locations. The sediment and bedrock that the creek erodes (the source for its sediment load) can differ substantially from place to place.

Figure 4.3. a) This deposit along the Mill River in Northampton, MA, contains cobbles and pebbles of many different types of rock. b) Close up of the Mill River deposit. c) The rock fragments in this deposit along the Jordan River in Bloomington, IN, are dominantly limestone.

Davis (2013a) contains a description of an exercise that involves describing and identifying the variety of rocks in a stream or glacial deposit.

T4.2. Track a place through the year.
Tracking a place through the year and observing how it changes with the seasons facilitates connection with yearly cycles in the behavior of plants and other wildlife, with how geological and ecological processes vary through the year, with weather patterns, and with other aspects of the place's unique character. The focus area for this exercise can be a local wildlife preserve, a public forest, an urban back yard, or another place where natural communities can be observed.

Note the times of year that different plants put their leaves out and when they flower. When do the various spring wildflowers begin to bloom? When does each species stop flowering and new species begin? Notice the differences in which animals are active and how their activity differs through the year. How does animal behavior change with season? Do the animals present in the area change with the seasons? Migrations of birds and insects play a role in the character of a place.

Part of my spiritual practice over the years has entailed regular visits to multiple natural places in the region where I live. One of these places in southern Indiana was the Scarce-o-fat Ridge Trail in Yellowwood State Forest. I enjoyed observing how high the creek was that I had to drive through to get to the trailhead, when the elder trees along the road were sporting white blossoms, and when their berries ripened. I would make a point to observe all of the wildflowers that were blooming in each season at different places in the landscape. I loved to be there during the blooming time of the first spring wildflowers such as cut leaved toothwort and spring beauty. I then enjoyed watching the changing of the guard, noting when nodding trillium appeared down in the floodplain of the creek and when the fleabanes were blooming along the old logging road. I loved seeing the naked flowered tick trefoil and whorled loosestrife bloom on the wooded ridgetop. I would note when I started to hear the spring peepers as well as when the maples, oaks, and hickories started to put out leaves. I have also enjoyed observing the seasonal changes along the Mill River, along Amethyst Brook, around Fitzgerald Lake, and on the slopes of Mt. Tom in Massachusetts. See Figures 4.4 and 4.5 for photograph comparisons between different seasons at two of these locations.

Figure 4.4. Mt. Tom at two different times of year, photographed from MA State Route 141 in Easthampton, MA: a) October 2012, b) February 2013, photographed from further away.

Weather, foliage, stream flow, wildflowers, and active wildlife vary with the seasons. Different species of plants of the forest floor grow, flower, and decay at different times of year. In a floodplain forest (Figure 4.5), the types of plants that are visible can vary from month to month.

a
b
c

d

Figure 4.5. Small creek feeding Fitzgerald Lake at four different times of year: a) March, b) April, c) September, d) November.

A generalized progression of blooming wildflowers in eastern North America is depicted in Figure 4.6.

Figure 4.6. Timeline of wildflowers photographed at eastern USA locations. The species present in each of the photographs (April in Indiana through September in Indiana) are spring beauty (*Claytonia virginica*), *Viola sp*, *Trillium erectum*, spiderwort (*Tradescantia sp*), pink lady slipper (*Cypripedium acaule*), St. John's wort (*Hypericum perforatum*), loosestrife (*Lysimachia sp*), Joe Pye weed (*Eutrochium sp*), giant ragweed (*Ambrosia trifida*), goldenrod (*Solidago sp*) and *Aster sp*, and common ragweed (*Ambrosia artemisiifolia*).

I highly recommend tracking places through the seasons as a way to stay in touch with nature in your area.

Natural landscapes also vary year to year. Differences in rainfall and water flow can affect a system or systems considerably. Changes can occur in multi-year cycles as well. For example, large numbers of cicadas come out of the ground in specific parts of the USA every 17 or 13 years. Many dead tree limbs were present several years after one of these outbreaks in the Bloomington, IN, area. In the Appalachians, gypsy moths have killed many trees on slopes and ridgetops, affecting those places for many years into the future. After devouring the vegetation on one mountain, the gypsy moth population moved on to devastate a neighboring mountain, and then onward to other places. A friend and I bushwhacked up Great North Mountain while the gypsy moths were feasting on the leaves of the canopy on that mountain. Their poop rained down on us as we ate dinner and then pelted the top of our tent through the night, adding to the ambiance of our experience.

T4.3. Track a place through day and night.
It can be illuminating to observe which animals are active at which times of day. This practice can include observing general bird activity times and the habits of particular species. Barred owls have been a friend to me in many landscapes over the years, especially when my dissertation field work in old fields continued into the evening hours and when camping.

T4.4. Delve into the infinite complexity, diversity, and beauty.
- Zoom into and focus observations on a small area (tightening spiral) and/or
- Zoom out to observe large scale complexity (opening spiral)

One can delve infinitely deep into a place and into a moment. When we focus on observing our immediate surroundings, we quickly realize that the place is complex and that many events are occurring. We can zoom into one small part of the immediate area and focus our attention there. This new smaller area comes into focus and has a great diversity of patterns, textures, and happenings. We can continue to zoom in, exploring the infinite wonder of the place. If we bring a magnifying glass or small microscope we can zoom in even further. What will a square millimeter of the forest floor look like under a scanning electron microscope? Figure 4.7 shows two photographs taken while zooming into a spot within the landscape.

Figure 4.7. Two photographs taken during the process of zooming into a spot in the landscape of an abandoned lot in Swansea, MA. a) Photograph of an area around a willow tree taken from a distance. b) Close-up photograph of the area that shows more detail regarding the branching and leaves of the willow tree as well as the seedlings and wildflowers growing under the tree.

You can zoom out from your immediate surroundings, slowly expanding your sphere of consciousness outward. What new things, perspectives, or interactions are entering your consciousness? Continue expanding the sphere of awareness outward, into the subsurface, out along the Earth's surface, upward and outward. This expansion of consciousness can provide a good jumping off point for a shamanic journey that may go in one direction, or multiple. The journey may or may not be obviously connected with your physical location within the Earth System (see the discussion of shamanic and meditative techniques in Chapter 7).

T4.5. Let the ocean pervade all the senses.
The ocean is a great place to delve into the complexity of a small place (a patch of sediment on the shore), or zoom out to the big picture. Watch and hear the ocean waves hit the shore. Smell the essence of the ocean in the air – breathe it in. Touch the sediments and the aquatic life on the beach.

Many methods and perspectives can be used to engage all your senses and many aspects of your consciousness. There are many ways of becoming aware of the diversity in nature, in a general sense or regarding a particular ecosystem. Connecting through maps and satellite images can be insightful as well as good training for viewing the landscape from multiple perspectives (broadening the sensory engagement and experience). It can be expansive and fun to imagine what the subsurface looks like in three dimensions. Geologists cultivate this skill to be effective at their work. We can also delve into experiencing various aspects of the living parts of an ecosystem and the interconnected web of life. We can experience the different kinds of insects in many settings (e.g., different types of dragonflies).

T4.6. Count different types of spiders in your backyard or other small area.
One way to connect with the diversity is to count types of a kind of wildlife. You can even do this in small urban yards. Spiders are a good choice because they are distinctive in appearance and have different types of webs or hunting styles. In the 1990s, in a 15 by 20 foot backyard in Northern Virginia, each of several seekers found on the order of ten different spiders during a period of several minutes.

Awareness of reproduction cycles and other types of animal behavior is another valuable way to connect.

T4.7. Watch animal behavior.
Many of us feel enlivened by watching wildlife. We have a curiosity about the natural world, and our emotional response can go beyond mild wonder as we feel our joy channels open. Whether it is watching a red tailed hawk eating a squirrel or a sparrow gathering materials for a nest, one can get into a trance through the experience – watching, listening, and smelling without engaging the analytical mind.

T4.8. Go birding.
Observing (looking and listening for) different types of birds captures the interest of many Naturalists. Birders get excited about how many birds they can find, and they keep track of which ones they see at particular times of year. When I talk with birders in conservation areas, they take delight in telling me which kinds of birds they have seen so far on their outing and which ones they have seen for the first time that year. Nesting habits are interesting to read about and to observe in the wild. Counting eggs for bird surveys can be done on a volunteer science basis, and so can identification of adult birds seen in an area. The number of bird songs and calls that you know is an unofficial measure of your experience and ability as a Naturalist.

"Nature is a great teacher. We are learning every day." Birder at Lake Fitzgerald

T4.9. Shine a flashlight down into a body of water at night.
Shine a flashlight into a lake or pond at night and watch until a bubble rises up
through the water column. Follow the bubble with your eyes and watch what
happens. I won't spoil the surprise for you.

Tracking lunar and solar cycles can also be very rewarding. Emotional states are tied
into the phases of the Moon – we feel it! The Sun also has a large planetary and
personal energy effect, many people experience more energy when the days are
long. People make conscious and subconscious observations of the Sun throughout
the year; and it can be fun to consciously note the change in sunrise and sunset
directions through the year, track the change in sunlight hours through the seasons,
and think about how the sunlight changes affect the rest of the system. Solar
holidays are celebrated today and have been celebrated by ancestors for thousands
of years.

I enjoy working with people who connect strongly with storms. We like to get out into
the storm, immerse ourselves in its energy, feel its pulse and movements, take it in
with all of the senses, track the storm with online maps and visually in the field, and
move between different parts of the storm. Hurricanes are very large, capable of
inhabiting entire states along the east coast of the USA all at once. My experience
with hurricanes has consisted of high winds and rain away from the coast, and I look
forward to a chance to witness a storm surge first hand. Tornadoes are incredible –
the way the conditions spring up quickly and the way they descend from the sky. The
warning signs are otherworldly. In western New York State in 2001, I was pelted with
hail moving horizontally at high speeds. I realized that I was inside a storm that was
more powerful than I had ever experienced, so I took shelter. After it passed, I
surveyed the damage to the campground where I was. Tents had been thrown long
distances, and there were linear strips of twisted off trees in the woods. A number of
years later I saw a funnel form and descend toward Vincennes, Indiana. It remained
suspended halfway between cloud and ground, never touching down. I marvel at the
lack of predictability as well as the intensity of the wind. Heavy rain, even without the
wind, can be intense. I will never forget huddling with a friend down in a small creek
bed among boulders during a downpour in Kentucky. We got an up close and
personal perspective on the processes involved with water flow into the stream from
in the ground and surfaces of the forest. Walking through snowdrifts while a blizzard
is happening is another special experience. I was blessed with a taste of this in early
2013 in Easthampton, MA. I was acutely aware of the swirling snow abrading my
face.

We relate to the weather daily, and we can take a breath to bring our awareness to it
in the moment. We can take a moment to feel the Sun. We can track rising heights of
streams, and even compare urban and natural streams, by collecting flow or stage
data during a storm. We can sense the link between rain and flood.

When making observations out in the field, published field guides are very useful. For
identifying wildflowers, I often use two guides: one with a decision key that can take
me through an identification based on flower parts and leaf arrangements [e.g.,

Newcomb (1977)] and a second with pictures for confirmation [such as Yatskievych (2000)] for Indiana and neighboring states. Internet resources have also served well as the confirming photograph reference. Useful plant identification references are available online [e.g., the USDA plant database (USDA, 2013)] and there is at least one smart phone application for identifying trees by their leaves. When identifying trees (and most other kinds of nature entities), it is best to use as much information as possible. Flower and fruit types, shape and size of leaf scars on the twigs, whether leaves are simple or compound, whether leaf edges are toothed, and the arrangement of leaves on the twigs are characteristics that support identification. During leaf-off conditions, twig, bark, and branching characteristics may all be necessary to identify a tree because each of these traits varies within individual species. Wojtech (2011) illustrates how bark can vary within and among a number of common tree species in the northeast USA. This field guide can help both beginners and experts recognize trees by the bark. The next chapter contains more resources for acquiring Naturalist knowledge through academic study.

Rappahannock
I come to the river
Blood flowing with its cadence
The current pulls me downstream
Flowing over crystalline rock
Wearing down
Old hills and hollows
Cobbles roll
Sand bounces
Mud floats
Traveling to their new home

Critters!!
Crawling, swimming, sliding
A larva rises through a deep pool
And moth emerges from the surface
Flying west
To the mountains
To help plants make love

Vein of earth
Life nexus
Feel all
Nurture all

O Mighty Rappahannock
Live in my flesh
Connect me to the world
Cut away the old and bring the new
I flow
I love
I listen for your song
                      Adam Davis, 2001 – 2009

CHAPTER 5. Academic study and Naturalist programs.

Academic study is another way of building an understanding of who and what to connect with in nature. Scholarship can provide background and context for what is sensed and experienced in the field. Combining multiple ways of knowing (e.g., the spiritual with the scientific, the empirical with the emotional, the sensory with the extra-sensory, and many other combinations of diverse approaches) can be made easier with background knowledge.

Through scholarship and research we can examine the Earth as a system, the materials it is made of, and the processes occurring within the system. The connections discussed in Chapter 2 can be examined from an intellectual perspective and through empirical investigation, and knowledge of cause and effect can be broadened through analysis of empirical data and scientific models. We can more comprehensively and thoroughly understand where our water comes from and where our body waste goes. We can understand the planetary effects stemming from how we create our energy and how we dispose of our garbage. Scholarship takes us beyond the concept of foodshed to reveal how we are linked into foodwebs within ecosystems. We can get better at estimating the size of our footprint by estimating it in diverse, multidimensional ways (e.g., in terms of hectares of land or in terms of kilograms of carbon).

College programs and courses can provide nature awareness. The combination of a Physical Geology (and/or Physical Geography) course and an Ecology course provides basics about how the Earth System works. Structural Geology coursework supports thinking in three dimensions and relaxation of temporal constraints. Historical Geology courses provide a sense of where we have been as a planet. Environmental Science teachings can show us the consequences of our actions within the Earth System. Botany and wildlife courses provide access to an immense wealth of information about patterns of wildlife behavior. You could take a course delving into trees. You could take regional landscape classes. You could take classes oriented toward flora and fauna of a specific area.

Extensive academic training in the Earth and environmental sciences is useful for developing a strong knowledge base concerning how the Earth works, solving environmental problems, wise land use planning, and responsible natural resource management. Studies in environmental policy and ethics, chemistry, social work, engineering, landscape architecture, folklore, economics, law, and agriculture are also helpful for assessing and avoiding environmental impacts, and moving toward sustainability. Multiple academic disciplines can be integrated to solve problems.

Outside of traditional academia, programs of study aimed at training Naturalists are available from a variety of sources: state and county conservation offices, free lance Naturalists, nature-oriented non-profit organizations, and diverse other sources.

In diverse areas of the USA, Audubon Society groups put on workshops and presentations on specific aspects of nature such as a visit to a blue heron rookery and a lecture on birds of prey. Local watershed groups and conservation agencies can provide useful resources and programs regarding wildlife behavior, threats to aquatic ecosystems, non-native invasive species, soils, and other aspects of the natural world. National and state parks often have full schedules of excellent programs during some seasons of the year.

Groups and agencies also work together to put on events, conferences, and workshops. Examples of these kinds of collaborations include spring wildflower forays held in Brown County, IN. These wildflower connection events have consisted of multiple full days of informative hikes in the forests and fields of southern Indiana. A three day Eagle Watch event, facilitated by a Department of Natural Resources Naturalist and private entities, has been a highly regarded multi-day event held in the winter along the shores of Lake Monroe, IN. Residents of southern Indiana have fond memories of eagle sightings around this lake.

Naturalists across the world facilitate ecosystem connectivity exercises and workshops open to the general public, and some work diligently to customize their events for programmatic goals, places, and participants. Both independent Naturalists and those employed by government agencies do consulting work aimed at helping people become more aware of their land and its natural resources.

Kids can learn Naturalist and wilderness survival skills through a variety of organizations and the programs that they facilitate: park and nature preserve summer camp programs, Boy Scouts of America merit badges (e.g., Forestry, Conservation, Geology), Outward Bound adventure programs, and more. Adult programs are also available in many places.

Private nature training schools for students of all ages exist across the globe. Some of these focus on broad Naturalist training and there are many that focus on wilderness survival skills. In the eastern and western United States, a number of schools introduce and engage students in learning about nature through use of mentoring techniques and have called their operational paradigm "the Art of Mentoring". Young et al. (2010) discusses core concepts and principles of the approach. To learn more about one of these schools, see Vermont Wilderness School (2007). More discussion about wilderness survival schools and resources for self driven survival study are provided in Chapter 18.

There are many sources of information available for self directed study. Landscape ecology, biogeography, and geoecology are among the many avenues of study that folks can follow after receiving foundational teachings in natural science. Nature and Geotimes are both useful periodicals. A great deal of information about the wonders of nature is available through the geological and natural resource agencies of states and countries as well as through national parks. For many of the U.S. National Parks, books have been written about individual aspects of the park ecosystem (e.g., wildflowers or geology) and usually one or two books link parts of the system together. Books with "natural history" in the title can provide a rich sense of the parts and/or workings of a particular ecosystem. Natural history books contain information about bedrock, soil, geomorphology, plant communities, other wildlife, weather, and more for specific regions and are fit for general consumption, digestible by most readers. These and a number of other publications weave information about many parts of ecosystems and landscapes together. Here are some examples:

- "California Landscape: Origin and Evolution" by Mary Hill
- "The Granite Landscape: A Natural History of America's Mountain Domes, from Acadia to Yosemite" by Tom Wessels

The Roadside Geology series is helpful for understanding the evolution of landscapes and nature of the bedrock for specific areas and along routes of travel – a separate Roadside Geology book exists for many US states.

Field guides are great to have with you in the field to help structure and augment observations as well as support identification. Also, field guides can be studied in preparation for field work. If you know what kind of observations to make, you can generate the right notes and take the right pictures in the field which can then be used later to identify plants, birds, rocks, or other nature entities.

Research is another way of connecting with the land. Inquiry into how aspects of nature work can involve collecting large amounts of field data and making many observations, can get you looking at the same place through the seasons, can get you to think about relationships, and can stimulate further inquiry. Research helps you look more into how natural processes work and/or get a sense of cause and effect in the system. Being out in the field for long periods of time on a research project provides spiritual benefits associated with immersion in the landscape energy (an expanded discussion of immersion is included in chapters 10 and 11).

My relationship with old fields and forests of southern Indiana was changed forever by completing three intensive field seasons, collecting many types of information, analyzing data with multiple techniques, and communicating my results in a variety of forums. I was opened to the connectivity in these systems, and at the same time was introduced to more and more of the mystery.

Citizen science is a way to participate in research efforts on a volunteer basis. Vegetation surveys, bird surveys, stream flow and water quality monitoring, and other projects are supported by data collected by volunteers. In the USA, stream monitoring workshops put on by local watershed groups, state natural resource or environmental agencies, Natural Resource Conservation Service offices, and other groups train volunteers to collect stream data. These workshops show participants the diversity of life within streams and possible variations in water chemistry. Other ecological and geological citizen science has been supported by the Nature Conservancy, the U.S. Geological Survey, and other organizations.

In summary, academic study can provide context for and methods for making nature observations. It can provide frames of reference for our spiritual work with nature. Scholarship can be incorporated into our experience in a way that does not narrow us into one way of thinking, naming, or categorizing. We can explore academic knowledge without elevating any discipline or teaching to being "right". Academic study can help us enrich our nature connections. It can provide vocabulary, conceptual models, and mental acuity for communicating and communing with the land.

CHAPTER 6. Conversations.

Conversations and interactions with nature entities can be like engaging with friends, acquaintances, or people you pass on the street. Dialogues can evolve as you get to know certain trees, rock exposures, entire landscapes, and/or other aspects of the natural world. Coming to a place for the first time is like going to a party where you don't know anyone. Your manner of interaction will likely be different than if you knew some folks, and it may change as you stay longer at the party or party with the same folks again in the future.

T6.1. Open to awareness of nature.
T6.2. Say hello.
T6.3. Show respect and reverence.
T6.4. Show intentions.
When first arriving at a place, I like to touch the ground or put a hand in the local stream and listen and feel. I often will introduce myself, state my intentions for being there, and show the energy/status with which I enter (i.e., level of respect and spiritual condition). Sometimes I chant the Lakota word "miyelo" meaning "it is me". I frequently use a three part prayer: "Thank you for who you are, I am willing to serve, I am open to your guidance". We can enter places with integrity and respect.

T6.5. Walk in silence.
Walking in silence can help us let go of obsessions of the analytical mind, and get us totally present in a place. It tunes us in to the smells, sounds, and sights of the place and can engage our intuition regarding pathways to travel.

T6.6. Listen.
Communicating with nature involves a quiet mind and enhanced awareness. Listening to the land and receiving its message(s) engages all the senses. The postures of the trees are saying something. The choruses of frogs, birds, and insects all paint a picture. Feeling how the energies of the place are interacting with your core is important communique from the land.

T6.7. Energy exchange.
We become aware of and intentional about how energy moves between our bodies and our environment. The energy exchange could have many different looks and feels, so there is an infinite amount of personal expression with this technique. I like to tune in to the place by squatting or kneeling to touch the ground and listening to see what energy exchanges are possible. As one of the common ways that I am intentional about energy exchange, I breathe in the essence of place and breathe out my essence. Another staple of my practice involves putting my energy down into the Earth and allowing Earth energy to come up into me – through hands or feet. Chapter 8 delves deeply into energy work.

T6.8. Explore synergy and mutual benefit as an ideal, and ask permission as a baseline.
Taking from the land without dialogue is stealing. Engaging beings of nature

intimately without asking permission is disrespectful. Ask and be prepared for a no answer. Ask the tree before leaning up against it. I ask before collecting a sample for my research or for teaching purposes. I ask before setting up camp, before taking water from a spring, and before lighting a fire. One time when I was scouting a site for a ceremony, I saw a fire pit and decided to check it out. As I got closer, I thought about what heat from a fire would do to the rootlets of a nearby sugar maple. I asked the tree for guidance and then got the idea to pour water between the tree and fire several times during the ceremony. It seemed that the tree offered me a way to give it respect and use that fire pit. On another occasion, I turned a strongly psychic friend onto the idea of using her talent to connect with trees. We were walking along a trail and turned to say hello to a tree, and I got a mild intuition that the tree wanted to be left alone. My friend recoiled, because she heard the tree tell us to leave it alone very strongly. Many beings of nature would rather be left alone.

The spirits of nature who are willing to work with us can provide information for having a successful experience. I check with the land and place before I lead a workshop or field trip in the area. I often get inspirations regarding what to emphasize and how to facilitate the event. I ask the land and aspects of nature what they want me to teach in my workshop. What do they want in ritual? What kinds of offerings do they like or are appropriate for the occasion at hand?

I consulted with multiple sites when looking for the place to do the Rites of Spring 2011 "Connecting with the Land" workshop. I received impressions that some places were not receptive to hosting our workshop, and others told me that there was a more appropriate spot. I iterated toward a location that ended up working very well for the workshop.

During a consult with the land in preparation for a summer solstice ceremony, members of Black Bear Grove (a Druid congregation) visited potential ritual sites along Lake Monroe in southern Indiana. A dead tree full of vultures was a prominent feature at one site while river birch saplings and young frogs were present at the other. The ritual theme of new beginnings seemed to fit better with the latter site.

T6.9. Offerings.
Praise offerings of various kinds can show gratitude and good intent to the spirits of the land. Giving gifts requires forward thinking intention, and is a sign of respect for the land. Biodegradable offerings that will not harm the land are ideal. Whiskey, cornmeal, incense, and tobacco are all common offerings from different traditions. The spoken word, song, and dance are also good ways of giving thanks and praise.

Offerings are stronger if they involve personal sacrifice. Something you really don't want to part with is more meaningful than something that you are looking to unload. An offering that involves personal creativity or a lot of care is more meaningful than something quickly and expediently obtained that was created by someone else or mass produced.

A place or specific nature beings can provide input regarding the offerings that are appropriate or preferred. At a ceremony at which the black bear was a guest of honor, berries were brought as offerings but not given during the formal offering period. An omen received later in the ceremony indicated that more offerings were needed and the group realized that the berries needed to be offered to the black bear.

T6.10. Bowing.
Bowing to an aspect of nature is a nice way to show appreciation and gratitude, and it is practiced by diverse traditions. While bowing with hands together in front, one can say the Sanskrit word "namaste" (I appreciate the divinity in you) like is done after a Yoga practice or kirtan. For some folks, bowing before entering a particular forest can be like bowing before beginning a martial arts practice or entering a place of martial arts work.

T6.11. Prayers.
Prayer is a ritualized way to convey intentions, marking the dialogue as sacred. Everything in this section could be considered prayers. A personal energy (and/or state) of reverence can be cultivated by the act of praying.

T6.12. Ask for guidance.
Dialogue with nature can result in guidance for life decisions. After pulling off of an interstate highway and going down to a stream near Washington, PA, I communed with a grove of silver maples on a sand bar along the stream and received a message to keep giving the "Connecting with the Land" workshops. On a sand bar in a Cleveland, OH, area river, I was told to write this book. It makes sense to me that I received information about steps in a longer journey while on the sand bars, since deposits in rivers are waypoints in the journey of the sediments. I was a grain of sand on the sand bar.

Part of my practice is to continually ask the land how best to serve. As I began clearing a designated ritual space at a nature sanctuary, I felt that my action was wrong for the land and found myself deciding to do it in service to my community anyway. I asked the nature entities and energies what I could do for them as payback for the disturbance that I was causing, and they suggested that I share my concerns with one of the planners of the ritual space.

It is very important to ask for guidance when choosing places for ceremonies, workshops, and field exercises. I like to meditate in a chosen site or walk along the route of a nature hike several days in advance and ask for input regarding ceremony/workshop/exercise content. I receive creative insights through this practice.

Communicating with all of the senses, will, and energy tends to support effective information exchanges. Geometric and spatial relationships are important components of nature's messages to us. Postures of plants and bird speech are both individual omens and part of the collective dialogue with the land that is possible, and happening whether we are aware of it or not.

T6.13. Oaths.

Pledges of service and lifestyle change can be ritualized and made part of group ceremonies or delivered as personal prayers. Oaths, pledges, and promises are given in many contexts by people of different backgrounds. The example included here is modified from the script of a dedicant oath given by a dedicant and taken by an oath facilitator (aka oath taker).

> FACILITATOR: Humans and deities present, bear witness to this rite of passage. Witness this oath of dedication to Earth, spirit, and community. Does the dedicant have a special offering for those who witness the oath?
> DEDICANT: I thank you all – deities, humans, ancestors, nature spirits – for coming to witness my dedication rite. I present you with 4 gifts – one from each chamber of my heart.
> FACILITATOR: Will you tune your spirit to the energies of the Earth and Universe?
> DEDICANT: I will.
> FACILITATOR: Will you serve the Earth and nature spirits?
> DEDICANT: I will.
> FACILITATOR: Will you serve human society as Naturalist and steward of the land?
> DEDICANT: I will.
> FACILITATOR: Will you fight the waste and disrespect of the beauty and riches of the Earth?
> DEDICANT: I will.
> FACILITATOR: Will you connect and work with your community in these capacities?
> DEDICANT: I will.
> FACILITATOR: What say the spirits? – *An omen was sought and the spirits indicated that the oath is received and that challenges lay ahead for the dedicant.*
> FACILITATOR Let it be so.
> ALL: So be it.

Folks may be held accountable for their oaths and pledges in one way or another, so I recommend taking this practice seriously and avoiding vague oaths or promises. I recommend making sure that any oath that you give is doable for you. If you fail to keep an oath, it is important to arrange a way to be accountable.

Sometimes mediation, condolences, or bearing bad news are part of the dialogue. I felt called to talk with a plot of land that was a suburban residential area being retaken by nature and that was slated to be redeveloped. Telling the land of the development plans was a depressing task.

Dialogue is an effective way to build relationships with animals, places, trees, bedrock, and others. We honor the truth of the ongoing relationships by saying hello, giving thanks, inviting, smiling, asking before intruding, and being otherwise polite.

CHAPTER 7. Meditative and shamanic techniques.

Quieting the mind, focusing on the breath, deliberate breaths into specific places in the body, breathing patterns such as those associated with Yoga and Qi Gong traditions (styles of breathwork are incredibly important meditative tools!!!), shifting consciousness, physical and shamanic travel, and alchemically transforming oneself while traveling are all very useful techniques for experiencing nature in a deep, multivalent way.

T7.1. Meditate in places in nature.
Sitting, standing, or laying down in nature and paying attention to the breathing can allow a unique awareness of a place to creep into your consciousness. Focusing on one spot with the eyes, listening to one sound, and hearing all sounds collectively are all helpful tactics for supporting a meditative trance. Meditative sounds abound in nature such as the rhythmic crashing of waves and babbling brooks. Yoga, ecstatic body postures, zazen, Qi Gong, and mantras also facilitate meditative states.

T7.2. Soft eye, ear, and nose techniques.
Soft eye techniques can be supportive of meditative and shamanic work. These eye techniques involve focusing on one location or locations while seeing elsewhere. This can be done by focusing on a frame of reference (such as index fingers held up in your peripheral vision) while the eyes are seeing in a forward or in-front direction. Another alternative involves staring at one feature (e.g., a pebble in a stream, or the boundary of a tree trunk) while seeing what is around the feature. Similar play with focus can be done with other senses such as hearing or smell.

T7.3. Breathe.
Breathing can be a great tool for encouraging a meditative state. There are many different systems and ways of focusing the breath that can customize a meditative state, support healing, facilitate cleansing, and help with other types of transformation. To support open meditation as part of nature connection work, I like to do a full body inhale for a comfortable amount of time, hold full, do an exhale that either takes the same amount of time as the inhale or is longer if I wish to cleanse and release that which doesn't support the work, hold empty, and then repeat this breathing pattern.

T7.4. Walking meditation.
There are many ways to do walking meditation. We can focus on the breathing while walking. We can also link breaths to the steps of the walk, taking a certain number of paces on the inhale, possibly a pace while holding full, exhaling for the same number of paces as the inhale, possibly taking a step while holding empty, and then repeating this pattern.

Walking really slowly is an excellent way to get a different sense about a place – to connect in a different way. Combine this with a light meditative state and impressions of the landscape can emerge in your mind's eye that are different from those that would emerge when you walk at your normal speed. Slowing down or speeding up can mark or highlight an area, allow your senses to be present with the energies of the place, and open the door to a deep connection.

Walking a labyrinth is a walking meditation that allows spiraling or meandering into the center of the labyrinth and then moving back out again. This is a way of working with the place while also doing personal transformation work such as letting go on the inward journey and manifesting something on a personal level on the outward journey. Figure 7.1 is an example of a simple spiral labyrinth in a natural area. The stones in the photograph are set up so that when we walk on the path between them we spiral in sunwise (clockwise) toward the center and then come out counter-clockwise. Other labyrinths are the reverse of this so that we clear and release while moving counterclockwise and then build or come into the new while going clockwise. In contrast to the simple spiral labyrinths, many labyrinths have a complicated pathway to the center that snakes back and forth. A labyrinth in the upper field of the Brushwood Folklore Center in western New York State has had multiple choices of paths – the journey takes different lengths of time to reach the center depending on the choices.

Figure 7.1. Spiral labyrinth in Amherst, MA.

Walking or dancing circles in the landscape can facilitate connection with what is in the center of the circle as well as encourage energy movement into or out of the circle's center. The energy flow is similar to that generated by dancing circles around a fire or tree as practiced at Native American powwows and Sundance, and at a variety of other celebrations and ceremonies across the globe such as the Free Spirit Gathering held in Maryland.

Guided visualizations (sequences of mental imagery, in many cases facilitated with spoken phrases) as well as sonically or otherwise driven journeys to natural areas or to meet specific nature beings can add dimensions to nature connection work.

T7.5. Journeys.
Journeys can involve communicating with guides and protectors beforehand and possibly during the experience. Journeying can be facilitated by certain frequencies of drumming (205 to 220 beats per minute) or other sounds (Harner, 1990). Ayahuasca, *Salvia divinorum*, DMT, and other hallucinogens can help facilitate as well (Harner, 1990), but some of these may be illegal in some localities. Protection, guidance, and multiple methods for returning from these kinds of journeys are critical for keeping these experiences helpful and healthy.

Folks who engage in these kinds of journeys (especially if new to the practice) use visualized conduits such as tunnels, caves, tree roots, tree trunks, paths, roads, railroad tracks, rivers, ridgelines, and smoke rising from a fire in addition to drum beats to travel through the landscape. Visualized conduits may relate to nearby natural features, and symbolic conduits or portals are components of the ritual spaces of multiple traditions. Energies and entities can come through these conduits to join the celebrants in their ceremony space and celebrants can use the conduits to travel elsewhere. Open planar areas can also play interesting roles in journeys. I like to journey on the top of thick flat clouds and to fly over the forest canopy.

You can use Basic Visualization Technique (BVT) to help "flip the shamanic switch" (see T3.4 in Chapter 3) to get started with journeying. When you find yourself journeying, you are likely in a unique type of trance that is open to interactions with energies and entities on many planes and, for me, is more work than a trance achieved with emptiness meditation. Harner (1990) calls this unique type of trance the shamanic state of consciousness (SSC). Pre-journey time is often spent forming the question(s), intention(s), and/or destination(s) as well as connecting with guides. Post-journey time is often spent reflecting and recording insights (e.g., journaling).

We can journey through natural areas remotely: tumbling down a river, soaring over the coast, ascending up to the cloud tops and moving laterally on the clouds. We can do multiple levels of journey and even journey on multiple planes at once. Local nature entities and energies can be engaged through this type of journey, as can beings from elsewhere.

T7.6. Engage landscapes via visualization, movement, and shamanic journey.
Visualization and journeying techniques can be applied to moving through the landscape at a particular location. Here are some examples:

- Tracing the horizon with your eyes while pivoting your body in a clockwise circle as your eyes move. In an enhanced version, you can go out to the horizon and interact with the space between you and horizon in multiple ways. This can be done in a group as a circle, everybody doing a solo spin in the circle.

- Two powers visualizations. These are commonly used visualizations for helping people prepare themselves for ritual activities. The consciousness and awareness can be led by spoken word outward from the body into the soil and rock below and then upward into the sky. These visualizations typically facilitate movement of energy from below and above into and through the body. It is a good technique for engaging in a deliberate energy exchange with the Earth and Universe. One common style involves imagining oneself as a tree, sending down roots, and then sending up branches. Regular, deep breathing for several minutes is recommended before beginning to move the consciousness through the landscape. The following is an example of words used to lead ritual celebrants through a two powers visualization:

  > Take a moment to become aware of the landscape around you.
  > Its hills and valleys, and its flora and fauna.
  > Feel the energy of the land.
  > Notice your place within the landscape.
  > And feel yourself begin to put down roots.
  > As your roots penetrate the soil, they soak up moisture and chemicals.
  > As they travel deeper, feel them flirt with crystalline basement rocks, tapping energy from the deeper earth.
  > Feel the earth's essence flow up through your roots and into your veins.
  > Notice your arms becoming more like branches of a tree.
  > Begin to extend your branches upwards into the sky.
  > Warming and nourishing yourself with the sun's rays.
  > As you become more and more like a tree, feel the other trees around you, your branches and roots mingling with theirs.
  > WE STAND TOGETHER AS A GROVE OF TREES!
  > (Davis, 1999)

  This mode of travel through the landscape can be used without a strict two powers focus. I use it regularly for exploring and healing. Corrigan (2000) provides a step by step guide for a two powers visualization.

- Going into soil and rock. A journey into a rock exposure or rock sample that you can hold in your hand can be the start of a dialogue with the rock. It can help you adjust your consciousness to be able to sense and communicate with the consciousness of a rock. Like many techniques in the book, I recommend doing it within a balanced spiritual practice. A friend of mine talked with a rock collection of hundreds of samples over a two week period and was altered significantly by the experience. She went from never doing it to mainlining the approach. I like her better now, but I advocate moderation with this and other techniques to ensure that they are ecologically sound for your circumstances. I advocate making sure that the techniques you implement contribute to a sustainable, healthy, and balanced spiritual nourishment. Occasional 15 minute chats with one rock at a time is likely more practical than what my friend did, especially if this is a new technique for you.

- Going into a tree (see Chapter 13).

- Journeying into the fire (I do not advocate doing this with the physical body).

- Visualize moving in the sky above the landscape and moving through it on the ground level at the same time. You can move in any geospatial pattern of your choosing, try it with more than two journeying perspectives, and/or combine it with the horizon exercise.

T7.7. Authentic wandering.
Travel through and engage with the landscape in an intuitive way, discovering and engaging energies and entities as you go. Authentic wandering involves nature awareness, following intuition, scanning for synergies, interacting and conversing with nature entities and energies, and physically moving through the landscape in an exploratory way that does not need to involve the analytical mind.

A trance state can be a helpful part of authentic wandering. A helpful trance state could involve presence in the moment, being plugged in to spirit energies, one with all, and an altered awareness that eludes words. An example of how a trance feels may be how you feel while meditating when you have gone a long time without your analytical mind recognizing a thought. Wandering becomes wandering when you are in a trance state. Communication with nature entities and energies can be a rich part of your travels through multidimensional landscapes.

Authentic wandering can involve many different forms of travel and consciousness. It can involve focus at specific places while also spreading awareness across the landscape. We can control the breadth of awareness and how we interact with each aspect of nature that we encounter. It can be cathartic to imagine flying from a high point like a vulture and/or crawling across the forest floor like an ant.

Figure 7.2. Journey through the wilderness around Cranberry Lake in the Adirondacks, NY.

One could forego cruising above the landscape via visualization or shamanic journey, and journey with a hang glider instead.

T7.8. Visualize communing and/or merging with beings and/or aspects of nature.
Visualizations that you internalize energetically can be a good way to plug in and do personal work. One example can be done when honoring the directions, the Earth Mother, and Sky Father as is done in Native American and Neopagan rituals. Visualize beings, things, and processes that occur in each direction and then visualize them coming into you. This is a way of defining your center and the ritual center. You are all of the beings that just came into you. For an added dimension, a physical action can be combined with the visualization such as reaching up and grabbing energy from a star.

Grounding may be desirable during or after the use of some of the journeying and trance techniques, and possibly more frequently desired in conjunction with the energy building and raising techniques, which are discussed in the book. Grounding can be accomplished by allowing the excess energy in your body to move out into the Earth.

Movements within formal or informal dances or martial arts are very meditative and trance inducing (Chapter 8 discusses two of these: the Tsalagi Dance of Life and a style of Qi Gong). Chanting is also a tremendous meditation aide. Certain words or tones that you can let resonate through your body (such as "Ohhhhmmmmm") can be repeated as mantras to encourage trance states.

CHAPTER 8. Energy work.

As mentioned in Chapter 6, energy exchanges of different types can be part of a dialogue with the land. Methods of moving energy or allowing energy to flow can be used to realize or forge nature connections. Sometimes we can see heat and other types of energy (including auras). Even if we cannot see them, energies are present. Energy can be focused by postures, mudras, symbols, and chanting. One example of energy manipulation is the practice of Reiki. In Reiki, Earth energy can be brought up through the body and out into the Universe. Then energy from the cosmos can be brought back down into the body and out through the hands. This energy is focused for healing purposes by symbols and hand posture. Reiki and other energy related healing modalities can be used to give energy to trees, other living beings, exposed rock, soil, and bodies of water. The energy from these methods can be given as offerings or as favors as part of a dialogue with the land.

T8.1. Move in circles.
Walking or dancing clockwise circles is a way to bring Earth Mother energy upward and is used in various healing practices. Clockwise circles can help us listen to the land and therefore improve our dialogue. Counterclockwise circles help us internalize the energies of experience or place (Casamira, 2013).

Energy flow can be enhanced by geometries in nature, such as in Sedona, AZ, and Bloomington, IN. A landscape underlain by flat-lying geology and featuring a continuous and strong rock formation exposed at a particular elevation, such as in the hills which surround Sedona and Bloomington, can provide an effect similar to that of a singing bowl, amplifying Earth energy and thus amplifying human healing powers and awareness. The amphitheater on the south side of Mt. Monadnock is another landform that has this amplifying effect. Chapter 9 discusses energies of the landscape in greater detail.

T8.2. Work with postures and movements that allow awareness and/or focus of energy movements.
Movements and postures from multiple traditions as well as those that are intuitively customized in the moment can support nature awareness and connections in diverse situations.

The Tsalagi Dance of Life (aka The Dance of the Seven Generations) is excellent for moving energy and sensing the whole landscape. I learned from Don Waterhawk to do the Tsalagi Dance in this way: face east, put out an eagle wing (extend right arm), then an owl wing (left arm), hug in energy from the east and take it down to the Earth, bring energy up from Earth and give it to the sky, bring energy down to center, extend an owl wing, then an eagle wing, gather from east, give energy to Earth, give to sky, bring energy to center, give back to east, transfer energy to the west, and then transfer the energy to center in the south. These same steps are then repeated starting in the south, then in the west, and then in the north. This whole process is repeated, moving through all four directions, seven times.

Qi Gong is another a way of moving and building energy. Qi Gong postures or movements can be accentuated by aspects of place as well as influence the awareness of place. The most memorable time that I stood in the "Twin Dragons out of a Cave" posture of the Taoist Elixir style of Qi Gong (Woods, 2001) was when I did so in a small, perfectly cylindrical, tunnel cave in the Deam Wilderness in southern Indiana on Easter Sunday. Resurrection!

I often synchronize energy exchange with my breath – a critical aspect of many energy practices like Qi Gong and Yoga. I like to breathe with my hands on the Earth. With my inhalation, I let Earth energy flow up into my body through my hands. With my exhalation, I allow energy to flow out through my hands down into the soil and rock. I combine this practice with the Tsalagi Dance of Life. During the dance, when my hands are on the Earth working with the Earth Mother, I take several extra breaths allowing energy to pulsate between me and the Earth. The Tsalagi Dance includes energy exchanges with the four directions as well as the Earth Mother and Sky Father.

Nature allies have supported me with cleansing energy releases, and I give gifts of my energy to nature entities and energies out of reverence, respect, and good intentions.

CHAPTER 9. Recognizing and working with energies of the landscape.

Each continent, region, and location is unique. Every ecosystem has its own processes, plants, animals, microclimates, and energy flows. Each place has its own essence and this essence has a unique effect on us.

The character of ecosystems varies from region to region and place to place. Biomes, ecoregions, and growing zones have been delineated based on types of living things in residence. EPA (2013) provides access to ecoregion maps of North America at numerous map scales. Even on the most detailed of these maps, there is a tremendous variety of individual ecosystems within each of the delineated regions. As an example of the variety possible, small (2 – 7 acres) old fields and forests have continuous variation in plant types and soils as well as having adjacent areas that are sharply different from one another (Davis, 2011). Detailed plant association and soils maps can provide an idea of some of the variations that are possible within ecoregions, types of forests, and otherwise identified natural systems. Geographical variations in living things can be linked to climate, bedrock and soil properties, land use history, water and air pathways, lay of the land, and other phenomena.

Plant communities vary with climate, elevation, slope angle and aspect, soil thickness and type (which relate to properties of the bedrock and/or sedimentary deposit from which the soil developed), the flow pathways of groundwater and surface water, and land use history (Davis, 2011). In ecosystems with similar land use history and slopes as well as similar climate (abandoned agricultural fields in south central Indiana), plant communities were found to vary within and among individual locations. Detailed research revealed that these fields contained different types of woody and herbaceous plants. Some of the differences were linked by Davis (2011) to subtle differences in the soils which were related to differences in bedrock type and water movements.

Figure 9.1. a) Old field (abandoned in the 1930s) located in Brown County State Park, IN, that features thin soils above siltstone bedrock. b) Old field (abandoned in the 1970s) that features soils of variable thickness above limestone bedrock located in the Griffy Woods Research and Teaching Preserve.

Relationships between parts of ecosystems are unique in specific regions and specific localities. Many workers have shown that a variety of factors influence the unique character of the landscape. I personally draw much inspiration from numerous distinctive regions across North America.

T9.1. Visualize a journey across a continent pieced together from memory and imagination.
Wearing the long wing feather as I fly, I fly above North America. I see the Blue Ridge with its round mountain outliers, including Old Rag Mountain in Virginia. I find a perch on Chimney Rock on Catoctin Mountain looking out over the foothills of the Maryland Appalachians. I roll with the hills of the Maryland and Virginia Piedmont, and I fly across the Chesapeake Bay and its many tidal tributaries. Circling back around and a little further south this time, I head to the Great Smoky Mountains and shelter in coves of ancient trees. From there, I fly northeast and then west across the Valley and Ridge Province (which features long ridges and long valleys) and then the Allegheny Plateau. The journey continues west through large expansive river valleys and agricultural ecosystems of the continental interior. Along the way, I flow through conduits and caves in southern Indiana. Moving to the northern Midwest, I soar with the bald eagles along the Mississippi River Gorge in Minnesota and then dwell in glacial terrain of the North Woods. Hail to glacial lakes, glacial sediments, black soil, pine, spruce, birch, loons, and moose. I glimpse the northern lights and sense the barren lands north of the tree line. From the plains of South Dakota, I dip down into prairie potholes, climb cliffs of layered sedimentary rock in the badlands, and move into the metamorphic and igneous rock of the Black Hills. These landscapes give way to buttes and table mesas, which resulted from the weathering of flat-lying sedimentary bedrock, in eastern Wyoming. Turning south and then flying west, I cross over mountains: the Colorado Rockies (Front Range and high peaks), then fault block mountains of the Basin and Range, and then the Sierras. Eventually, I take a dip in the Pacific Ocean – feeling its tall, powerful waves. To the north, the coastline is rocky with steep cliffs and natural terraces. Starfish can be seen among the rocks in the tidal zone. Circling around, I fly a southern route across mountains of Arizona, spiraling in among the spires of Cathedral Rock and Bell Rock in Sedona and soaring on air currents that follow pathways of glaciers and ancestral rivers. After moving east over arid and then humid Texas, I encounter the Gulf of Mexico. I swoop low along the gulf coast and say hello to the muds of the past and present Mississippi deltas. Hail these landscapes and others such as the Hudson Valley and Catskills; mountains of northern New York, Vermont, and New Hampshire; and rift basins up and down the east coast such as the Deerfield Basin, Newark Basin, and Culpeper Basin. Hail the diverse beauty of the landscapes and ecosystems of North America!

Mountain chain character varies from place to place. The Appalachians are lower in elevation than the Rocky Mountains, because the last Appalachian mountain building episode was much longer ago. Natural forces, such as water flow, have had more time to wear them down. The peaks of the Adirondacks and Sierras are rounded, consistent with granitoid bedrock, while some of the mountains in Vermont have sharp peaks with steep slopes consistent with layered metamorphic bedrock. In the Valley and Ridge Province of the central Appalachians, the terrain is characterized by long linear ridges separated by valleys. The lay of the land is influenced by faster weathering (break down of rock over time) of limestone compared to sandstone. These rocks were folded during a tectonic collision with Africa, and the resulting rock structure influenced the shaping of the landscape we see today.

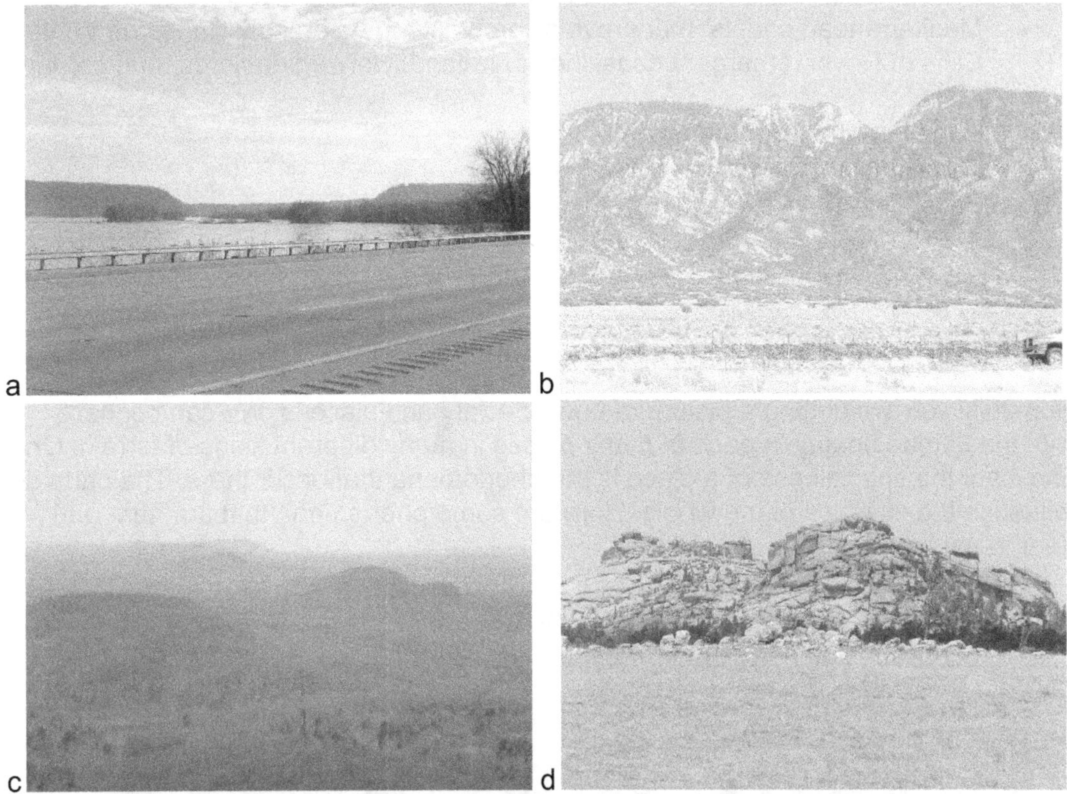

Figure 9.2. The differing character of mountains. a) Gaps occur in the Valley and Ridge Province of the Appalachians where the larger rivers (e.g., the Susquehanna River in the photograph) were able to cut through the sandstone bedrock over time. b) A steep mountain range at the edges of a flat valley typical of the Basin and Range Province. c) Slopes in the Holyoke Range parallel the tilt (dip) of ancient basalt flows. d) A ridge in Wyoming that is rounded due to spheroidal weathering of the granite bedrock.

John McPhee steadily covers the underlying geologic character of the landscape across the continent through a series of novels (McPhee, 1998).

Exploring the overall character of regions on all of the Earth's continents is a task for many lifetimes. Here is a list of places and phenomena I would love to experience:
- Taiga and tundra of Siberia.
- Glaciers of Alaska and Greenland.
- Islands of the Caribbean.
- Mountains: Alps, Andes, Atlas Mountains, Himalayas, Canadian Rockies, and more.
- Plateau and steppe regions of Tibet and Iran.
- Tropical rain forests of South America and Asia.
- Terraced plantations in Asia and Lebanon.

- River systems: Ganges (especially its delta and headwaters), Amazon, Nile, Elbe, and others.
- Old rocks of India, Africa, and Australia.
- Deserts of the Middle East, Africa, S. America, and Australia.
- Mediterranean coasts, mangrove swamps along Asian coastlines, the White Cliffs of Dover, emergent coastlines in Ireland, Norwegian fjords, and coral reefs.
- Karst terrain of Southeast Asia.
- The tide coming in in the Bay of Fundy.
- Basalt flows of Hawaii.

What does your list look like?

Sacredness of places

Hopefully you are getting a picture of how special each place is. We can connect with the unique beauty in each of many places in many different kinds of terrain. One aspect of the specialness of a place is the phenomena that occur there. The parts do influence the essence of the whole. Here are some phenomena that are near and dear to my heart:

- Spanish moss growing on live oaks.
- Crystals of ice propping up soil.

Figure 9.3. Freezing and thawing of water moves soil and rock.

- Springs where water flows from the ground into a stream on the surface.
- Wetlands. They display a vibrancy of life and remind me of the joys of a swamp walk. The high water table and sediment lead to preservation of fallen

plant material. The variety is tremendous – peat bogs, cypress swamps, and coastal marshes are well known types. I enjoy the small wetlands in the floodplain of my local creek.

Figure 9.4. Wetland of southeastern Georgia.

- Streams of almost any kind. The diversity among creeks and rivers as well as commonalities in structure and behavior (such as riffles and pools, or meandering) fill me with a sense of wonder.

b

Figure 9.5. Two creeks that meander (move side to side establishing a curvy channel), and have riffles (shallow rapids) and pools (deeper areas where water moves slower). a) Amethyst Brook in Amherst, MA. b) Griffy Creek in Bloomington, IN.

- The shaping of the landscape by running water or glaciers is very inspiring for me. Water, gravity, and time carve gullies and steep valleys in the highlands, rills (small channels) in exposed soil, and deep canyons.

Figure 9.6. Canyon carved by the Little Colorado River.

- Mountain summits, ridges, and slopes. Mountain laurel that grows on the shoulder of the ridges and hills in the Appalachians is a very prominent part of the character of these mountains. See Figure 12.5.
- Disturbed ground, abandoned mines, and other desolate landscapes.

Figure 9.7. Seeps of acidic water along the side of a pile of coal mine waste in Bicknell, IN. This seepage contributes to what is considered "acid mine drainage". Conditions in affected soil and streams can be too acidic for most forms of life.

- Many different wildlife habitats occurring within a landscape: the edge of a forest where it intersects a field, deep forest, young forest of an abandoned field, gaps in the forest canopy, floodplain, midslope, ridgetop, and more.
- Various stages of succession – the progression of vegetation types that occurs after cleared or barren land is left alone.

What natural phenomena spark your curiosity, fill you with wonder, and/or engage your heart? Do you have ongoing relationships with specific places? Have you been deeply impacted by a particular place in the past? A special mountain view? A quiet place along a creek or river?

Uniquely sacred places are everywhere. I feel blessed to have the opportunities to connect with beautiful and powerful places in a variety of landscapes. Each place has power that engages the spirit. An old field in Indiana, rows of pine trees on a small hill in western NY, and an abandoned coal mine in Wilkes Barre, PA, all provide symbolic meaning and nourish me, even as I am also enlivened and renewed by the power of mountain tops and tranquility of stretches of rivers and creeks.

As discussed in Chapter 3, each being and place possesses individual energies and a unique overall energy. Energy is transferred (flows) through the landscape and collects in certain places. The spatial pattern of energy conduits and concentrations is unique to each landscape, and this pattern influences happenings in the local ecosystem and human states of being. Energies in these places have potential to influence diverse phenomena and can be tapped intentionally for various efforts. Their capacity to influence lives, endeavors, and more can be called power.

Powers of place and our relationships to them vary. Some spots may be great for contemplation or meditation while others may aid in healing. They may be conducive to magical workings – personal and group ritual. The nature of the power is shaped by many interrelated factors: metaphysical properties of beings (living and non-living) that dwell there, geometrical configurations of land masses and water bodies (Champoux, 1999), energy patterns and movements, astronomical alignments, lines of power in the landscape that are similar to meridians identified in the human body by acupuncturists, and other factors.

Since each place has its own unique energy and energies, which can be complex and mysterious, attempts to get to know the energies of the land can benefit from use of all the senses, intuition, and philosophical dexterity. I suggest looking for (or at least being open to the possibility of) energy exchanges, conduits and other linear features, linear patterns of flow, places with circular flows, and geometric relationships between features in the landscape.

In some cases, energy conduits may be highly evident. Sometimes, specific locations or spots that are enhanced in a particular quality will be noticeable (some call these "power spots"). You can find these power spots if you or someone you are with is sensitive to land energies. This energy sensitivity may be naturally stronger in some folks than it is in others, and it can be cultivated and maintained through a regular spiritual practice and good physical health. I suggest maintaining awareness of energy flows through the landscape regardless of whether you have identified power spots, because these flows can give you context for power spots and help you understand the whole landscape. Specific postures may help with the identification of specific flows and determination of their character. Certain mudras and full body postures of a variety of traditions tune us in to certain energies, and you can intuitively shift your body into the posture that helps you sense a particular aspect of the place. For example, you could position your body in a way that helps you connect with the bottom of a lake.

Air and water flow patterns have energetic effects. Differences in the patterns translate into magical or metaphysical properties. For example, in Johnstown, PA, the mountains hold up the air on the windward side of ridges of the Allegheny Mountains which allows for a pause and transfer of qualities brought in by the wind.

Diverse physical channels in the landscape affect energy flows (past and present):
- River or creek (these may have multiple channels depending on the flow)

- Valley or ridge
- Tree (trunk, branches, and/or roots)
- Caves and sinkholes in karst terrain (landscape developed by weathering of limestone over time)
- Fractures and faults in the bedrock

Energy flows linked to mass movements and energy transferences include warm and cold fronts, mountain and valley breezes, sea and land breezes, insolation, heat radiated from Earth, water flow underground and in channels, and rock and soil sliding down a hillside. Imagine the movements happening in your landscape.

Observable properties and features of an ecosystem are related to its metaphysical and spiritual characteristics. The character of a place can invoke emotions, and inspire us on psychological and spiritual levels. Understanding physical-emotional-spiritual linkages helps us sense energies and powers of the landscape. Knowledge of the possibilities can validate small hunches or gut feelings that we might otherwise ignore.

The powers of the land may be aligned with certain types of inspirational or ritual work that you would like to do. Although each place does need to be treated uniquely, some generalizations can be useful.

Certain places are good for projecting something out to the world or sending energy to a specific being. Noses (curved ends of ridges) are good places to project from. Also, sending energy and the intentions of prayers can be facilitated by long straightish conduits [mountain ridges, long rivers, railroad tracks, or long ley lines (a "ley line" is a straight line that connects historical structures and markers)].

Healing, protection, and looking inward are well facilitated in valleys. Coves, basins, or low areas surrounded by hills or mountains can amplify healing powers and powers of intuition.

A creek or river with braided channels can be a good place for encouraging the integration or weaving together of various threads of existence. The confluence of two major rivers is generally a good place to do this, especially if there are exactly two patterns that you wish to bring together.

Vortices, circular energy patterns with flow of energy in and out, occur regularly in certain landscapes (e.g., various places in the Sedona, AZ, area), and during storms. The vortices can result in the creation of synergies as energies are swirled together.

One reason that places can support specific prayers or ceremonial goals relates to what is known as the law of association in magic. According to this law, properties associated with a place can inspire the same sorts of results in our personal efforts (Bonewits, 1971). For example, an area in the landscape with a throng of vibrant, diverse plant communities would be a good place to ritually usher in a period of growth for many aspects of our lives.

Exploring the idea of power lines, we can visualize networks of these lines as veins and nerves of the planet. Meridians identified by Chinese medicine in the human body are a good analogy for power lines in the Earth. Chakras in human bodies are a good analogy for power spots of Earth [see Brennan (1987) for maps of the chakras in the human body]. Where are the Earth's chakras? Does their location relate to the magnetic field or the thickness of the crust (which relates to mountain chains)?

Reading about lines of power is a way to learn about possible expressions of linear patterns, and references can support evaluation of whether a named ley line or ley marker (an indicator of the presence of a ley line) is present at a place or in a region where you are connecting. Ancient-Wisdom (2013) indicates relationships of identified ley lines to astronomical alignments, the Earth's magnetic field, and funerary paths in the British Isles. In this excellent summary, the authors consider dragon currents (the basis of Feng Shui), the fairy paths of the Irish, and ley lines to be based on or referring to the same type of lines of power. Ley lines connect megalithic sites and often correspond to springs and other water sources. Roads and other human structures (modern and of antiquity) spatially correlate with ley lines as well. See Ancient-Wisdom (2013) for maps of European ley lines, and See Champoux (1999) for mapped ley lines of North America. Multiple cultures seem to have worked with lines of power through sacred sites and sacred geometries associated with the landscape. Champoux (1999) suggests the possibility that the founding fathers of the United States of America used their knowledge of sacred geometry to focus the power of the North American landscape for the purpose of creating and preserving the nation.

I believe that the easiest way to find power lines or power spots in the landscape is not to look for them and more or less stumble upon them instead. I believe it to be most effective to sense and work with the essence of a place. If power spots are present, their locations can emerge through the use of shamanic, meditative, and energetic techniques while wandering the land.

During one of my visits to Sedona, AZ, I wandered around in a shamanic state of consciousness (see Chapter 7) connecting with the land. I was feeling the vibe of the landscape, and I ended up desiring to spiral (circle inward or outward) or rotate my body at certain places, usually at a particular elevation where a resistant sedimentary rock layer created small flat shelves on the sides of the buttes that surround Sedona. More wandering revealed these spots as energy eddies. My feeling was that they are relicts of past energy flows of ice and water in combination with modern air flow patterns. Trees twist with these energy eddies. You can feel the energies in your intuition when authentically wandering. **T9.2. Go to Sedona.**

It is often helpful to use a combination of intuition, empirical investigation, and the counsel of others (in person, print, computer, or phone) when investigating the energies of a place. You may be walking the land and stumble upon a place that feels special, and your intuition may even tell you that the place is acclimated to particular activities (e.g., it feels like a gathering place, feels like a place where significant religious ceremonies were held, etc.). If you look closer, look on old maps, or talk to old timers and historians you may find out that indeed that place was an important gathering place, or was the site of Native American ceremonies. A friend and I visited a Native American ritual site currently in use on a power spot on high ground on a Potomac River terrace. The combination of historical significance and modern channeling is generally enlivening, can help you understand and develop feelings of empathy or love for the place, and may impart specific inspirations. You can connect with the ancestors of the land.

Power spots of various sizes have been sensed and honored in various ways subconsciously or consciously by past cultures, and they sometimes are sensed and honored in present cultures. Structures may have been built to mark and accentuate the sacred spaces. We can see relics of some of these today: mounds in the midwestern USA (e.g., in Knox County, IN, 3 of approximately 300 mounds were still intact as of 2007), Serpent Mound in the state of Ohio, stone circles of the UK, and ley markers that indicate the paths of ley lines. Lake-Thom (1997) indicates known power centers (whole landforms or natural areas with elevated spirit energy) around the globe and in North America (e.g., Machu Picchu, Mount Shasta, and Niagara Falls), and offers good techniques for exploring and working with them. Lake-Thom (1997) also provides references that can help us tap into the cumulative knowledge base of generations of shamans that have worked with power centers.

Sometimes old or modern pathways of humans and animals can be sensed through shamanic techniques. The current pathways can be intuited or we can be led subconsciously into following them. The trails along Amethyst Creek in Amherst, MA, are braided in a way that looks as if the human walking patterns were inspired subconsciously by the braided channels of the creek.

Different energies occur in the landscape at different times of day. The energy before the dawn, the energy with Sun in the east and birds singing, the energy at dusk, and the energy in the middle of the night all have their unique qualities. The time between the seasons, and the time between the phases of light and dark leave unique imprints on the character of a place.

Connecting in death, and rebirth of nature relationship

We connect with the land based on where we are buried or scattered when we die. Burial customs shape this relationship. For this reason, I do not want to be sealed in a vault. I want to be able to go back to nature.

Landscape position, stones chosen to mark the graves, and planted trees all have cultural significance. Rough natural stones are strong and powerful markers, but the workmanship in ornately engraved stones is also impressive. Figure 9.8 shows rough hewn stones marking the resting place of an ancestor of mine in an old cemetery located on a nose in Worcester County, MA. Yews are planted in the lower part of this cemetery. The Yew represents renewal as well as long life. Cedars are planted in other areas based on a similar symbology.

Figure 9.8. Old cemetery in Worcester County, MA. The evergreen trees in the top left portion of the photograph are yews.

Where we are buried within the landscape affects how we experience the land. According to family legend, one of my ancestors did not want to be buried near his kids, because he did not want to get his feet wet (Phillips, 2011). He was buried in a landscape position which has different hydrological conditions than the landscape position of his descendants. Cemeteries seem to be located in upland areas more often than down in floodplains. Perhaps the living know that the dead do not want to spend time submerged under water.

T9.3. Get out into nature and sense the energies of the land and the sacredness of place.
Visualize or physically go to a place that you regularly visit. How does it differ through the day? What kind of spaces and energies are there? Where are the highs or lows in elevation, the channels, and the power spots? What types of trees are there? Do you have intuitions to engage in dialogue with any part of or being in the place? Are you drawn to a particular spot within the area? Are there pathways you feel called to follow through the place?

As examples of the sacredness and power of place, I offer my reflections about the energies of special places I have frequented as well as personal or group work that I may have done there:
- Pine forest behind a church in the Town of Aurora, located in western New York State. This was one of my first sacred spaces, a place I went for solitude and contemplation when I was young. This topographic low point, populated by rows of planted pines without understory vegetation, was at the intersection of opposite facing slopes. The journey through thickets to get to this wooded area likely enhanced the tranquility I felt there. The power of a place is influenced by the character of adjacent areas.
- American beech grove in Chestnut Ridge Park. The size of the beech trees and carpet of moss that was the forest floor gave this place an ethereal quality. An old natural order was present.
- Potter's Falls. Swimming up under the falls and feeling the water cascade

over me has been beyond refreshing, and I have felt clean and clear after swimming and sunbathing on large flat rocks downstream from the falls.

- Allen's Creek, its valley, valley side, and ridge. Foundational ritual sites for Black Bear Grove, location of a sugar maple under which the grove conducted rituals and under which I have done personal fire work, a field from where I got my hickory staff, a large guardian oak that watches over the valley, and a fairy corridor on the ridge are all aspects of this place. At the end of a peninsula, where Allen's Creek meets the larger part of the Monroe Reservoir in Indiana, there is a beach with crinoids that was a favorite meditation spot of mine when I lived in the region. Wandering around the entire peninsula that juts out into Lake Monroe at that location provided many hours of nourishment, connecting with spirits, and learning.
- Nose along the Grubb Ridge Trail. This nose is in the Deam Wilderness of Hoosier National Forest. The surrounding wild forest can be felt strongly when camping on this topographic high. It has been a great place to project from during ceremonies and magical workings.
- Hickory nose near Griffy Lake was a place at which I would ask the local spirits for guidance. I led a ritual to work with the local spirits at this place.
- Cooper's Woods in Vincennes, IN. This floodplain forest along the Wabash River has vestiges of multiple past human landuses, a large bur oak with whom I liked to talk, and the meandering Kelso Creek flowing toward the Wabash River.
- Oubache Trails Park in Vincennes, IN. Sandstone exposures along small creeks, wetlands, loess cliffs, both mature and young forest, and the banks of the Wabash River are features of this park.
- Leonard Springs. The water comes out from the hillside through fractures in the limestone and flows out from a cove into a wetland nestled in among rolling hills of the karst terrain of western Monroe County, IN. The site has the physical characteristics and the feeling typical of karst in that part of Indiana. Due to the topography and layering of different types of limestone, the site has a comforting combination of energy patterns.
- Rapids area along the Mill River in Northampton, MA. The conditions here are excellent for meditation and healing. The music of the rapids has a calming effect. Focusing on a boulder, another point in the stream, or on the banks can facilitate moving into a meditative trance. I like to stand in the river and visualize water flowing through me and cleansing me.
- Beech along Amethyst brook, Amherst, MA. This beech marks an excellent spot for meditation, chakra clearing, and exploration of healing postures.
- Billy Goat Trail along the Potomac River. Walking across a tremendous diversity of rock types and feeling the flow of the river through Mather Gorge activates all my senses, my emotions, and my whole spirit.
- Paint Branch Creek, College Park, MD. I received much nourishment from walking and sitting along this creek, especially at the confluence with Indian Creek. The character of the gravel of the creek bottom was notably different from the shale fragments and fine grained muds in the creeks of western New York State where I had previously lived.
- Prince William Forest Park. The site of group connecting exercises at the

Trillium Gathering. I love the bedrock of this park. This mysterious rock has been called a "mélange", likely formed by many processes acting together. The diverse landscape of the park is precious, featuring both broad upland areas vegetated with deciduous forest and narrow ridges with pine trees.

- Old Rag Mountain. The climb to the top, the descent, and the relationship developed over many visits to Old Rag have greatly shaped my character.
- Overlook along the Metacomet-Monadnock Trail in the Holyoke Range southwest of Mt. Tom. The link between the mountain range form and tilt of the ancient basalt flows is clearly observable. This place has helped me decompress. I can take off from the summit and fly over the forest canopy below.
- Woods behind my childhood home in Orchard Park, NY. My brother and I would play in a drainage ditch/creek at the edge of the woods. A neighboring kid took us on our first bushwhack, following the creek through underbrush and into the forest. There were old fields nearby as well, and I remember walking back past an old car on family walks. This place provided teachings regarding the dynamic nature of landscapes and influences of past land uses.
- Pioneer Mothers Memorial Forest near Paoli, IN. I have enjoyed visiting this patch of old growth forest to experience five foot diameter black walnut trees and an old natural order that can be felt coming up from the forest floor.
- Mountain near Laconia, NH. On this mountain, one of my oldest friends and I feasted on the most flavorful blueberries either of us had ever tasted.
- Point in Lake Accotink. This peninsula was a favorite meditation spot the first time I lived in Virginia. A great blue heron added to the picture perfect tranquility of this location. This magnificent bird was a regular companion.
- Griffy Lake. Several places overlooking the lake were popular meditation spots, and trails were important for walking meditation. I went to these places to recharge, for companionship, and to fortify my relationship with self. These places preserved my sanity during my dissertation process.
- Each of the six abandoned agricultural fields (young forests with some remaining open areas) in southern Indiana that were the subject of my dissertation. I led connecting exercises at three of these locations, opening my mind to new techniques. I walked, sat, and did two powers visualizations at each site many times. The fields were regular parts of my personal practice for over five years. I sat and listened to the barred owls call back and forth at dusk, received turtle and snake omens, and learned many plants and wildflowers. I worked with the Sun, orchids, and my guiding spirits. Doing regular work in these old fields kept me in a "plugged in to nature" state perpetually while I lived in Bloomington, IN. Many other gifts, including a Ph.D. degree, were bestowed upon me through working in these fields. Many thanks, old field spirits of south central Indiana!!!

What contributes to the sacredness of place? Lay of the land; heat transfer; resident beings; energy flows; chemical reactions; water pathways and flow; air pressure and movement; soil dynamics; our physical, mental, emotional, and spiritual state; and much more give a place its unique character. Hail the mysterious essence of the land!

CHAPTER 10. Immersion in nature.

"The wild nurtures our souls" Wilderness Society

Physical journey through the landscape is my favorite activity. I love to walk, hike, wander through rivers, saunter along mountain ridges, and hoof it up and down the sides of ravines. "And miles to go before I sleep" (Frost, 1923). I like to change speeds – go fast and then slow down dramatically to mark a place, to change perspective, and to open my senses to the energy of the place. I also find it extremely enlightening to stay in one natural location for various lengths of time and immerse myself in the essence of that place.

Immersing oneself in one or more aspects of the landscape can complement meditative techniques. The more intense or raw the immersion is, the easier it is to be fully present in the place we physically inhabit. The illusion of separation between us and nature can be dissolved. We are the creek in which we swim. We are the mountain we climb.

Here are some of the activities that can facilitate raw immersive experiences:
- **T10.1. Swimming.** One of my favorite ways of being fully present is swimming in rivers, creeks, lakes, and oceans. Submerging in a cold mountain stream during the spring season makes me feel intensely alive, clean, and mentally clear. This practice resets my spirit.
- **T10.2. Climbing a mountain.** Changes in the landscape on the way up a mountain leave their mark on the journey. Their essences are imprinted on my psyche. After having carried our packs for a full day on the Appalachian Trail, a friend and I had the choice to stay at a hotel and partake of a delightfully smelling barbeque or press on to reach the top of Springer Mountain – the southern end of the trail. We chose to hike on, arriving at the summit with the last light of dusk. We made it! Old Rag Mountain is a challenging yet increasingly popular day hike near Sperryville, VA, that has been a regular climb for me. Half Moon Mountain near Wardensville, WV, is also one of my favorite climbs. Wandering around a high mountain meadow and lake below Mt. Bierstadt is a good way to experience the essence of the Colorado Rocky Mountains as well as terrain shaped by Alpine glaciation. I get into an interesting emotional state when I bushwhack straight up the sides (no switchbacks, no trails) of mountains – Great North Mountain and Feedstone Mountain in Virginia come into my memory – hiking up through laurel thickets. Mt. Washington near Old Rag and a ridge within the Clifty Falls Wilderness in Kentucky were similar beelines straight up the mountain. While backpacking through a wilderness area within Pisgah National Forest in North Carolina, a buddy and I did what felt like a marathon straight up the side of a ridge – it was steep and kept on going. We were relieved to reach the top. At the summit of a climb, elation and contentment can be part of the experience, and views can be inspiring. Seeing the landscapes for many miles into the distance allows for a deeper awareness of the region and a sense of the majesty and infinite mystery of the Earth. Mt. Bierstadt in

Colorado and Mt. Monadnock in New Hampshire come to mind as having been particularly powerful summits for me. The shapes of mountain peaks and ridges, the terrain in front of us as we climb, and the scenic views are all joys of climbing a mountain. I give thanks to the mountains:

> Mountains of North America, thank you for your majesty and your charm, for the journey and the joy, and for diverse character and beauty. Hail to the Wallowas, Smokies, Blue Ridge, Holyoke Range, Berkshires, Green Mountains, Adirondacks, Ozarks, Catalinas, Sangre de Cristo Mountains, Basin and Range, Rockies, Sierras, Alleghenies, Valley and Ridge, Cascades, and all the rest. Hail the Mountains of North America.

Figure 10.1. View from Catoctin Mountain. Photograph taken from near Chimney Rock, December 31, 2007.

- **T10.3. Bushwhacking.** Going off trail and making our own paths through the landscape helps us get in touch in a raw and primal way. By bushwhacking down through a "rhododendron hell" in North Carolina, a buddy and I got acutely in tune with the reason for the "hell" part of the nickname. Sliding face first down the mountain under the dense rhododendron and laurel shrub layer also got us in touch with the soil of the rhododendron covered slopes of that part of the Appalachians. Climbing to the summit of Generations Mountain through laurel thickets in North Carolina was another rewarding bushwhack. Walking through old clearcuts in Dolly Sodds Wilderness, the Great Smoky Mountains National Park, the Poconos, or other eastern balds can involve hiking through dense shrubs. Wandering through these places can facilitate awareness of what the absence of the large trees can mean for mountain top vegetation.
- **T10.4. Trail running.** Running through woods and dodging obstacles (branches, tree trunks, boulders, etc.), focused and present, can shift energy and provide a perspective change.
- **T10.5. Hopping from boulder to boulder in a stream.**

- **T10.6. Talus surfing.**
- **T10.7. Bouldering/climbing a cliff.** Past near death experiences, almost falling from cliffs, have come to mind when I am at a challenging juncture in a climb, making the experience even more emotionally exhilarating.
- **T10.8. Climbing a tree.** Physically climbing up into a tree is a great way to gain a different perspective. The climb provides a deeper understanding of the way a tree has grown. Being up in the tree, we have a local aerial view and at the same time are invisible to many beings moving on the surface that don't look up. There is a sense of being apart from and hidden from others. The tree provides safety. Animals climb trees to escape danger, as have humans to escape bears.
- **T10.9. Walking barefoot.** Many feel more connected with the Earth when they go without shoes. The skin on the bottom of your feet helps you be more aware of the different textures of the ground you walk across. Bare feet also makes you aware that each substance has a different albedo (ability to reflect sunlight). Black rock and black top are hot! Cleansing with Earth energy, grounding, connecting with Earth divinity, and other energy work can be encouraged and supported by walking or standing while free of footwear.

We are working with the land energy on many levels when we use these techniques. There can be a noticeable shift in the state of our body, mind, and spirit when we arrive and become present with the space. Getting there and deepening into the place facilitates feelings of kinship and oneness with the land. We can further explore or enhance the oneness by employing, following, or allowing meditative techniques while we are immersed in the wilderness. Be the place. Be the woods. Be the river – flow spirit flow.

T10.10. Tune to nature's music.
Running water and other nature music can set our brain waves to enhance or initiate a meditative state. We can use authentic movement (or authentic wandering) and intuitively flow with the energies without thinking. I like to imagine the river flowing through my body and cleaning out my chakras, impurities, blockages, and barriers.

T10.11. Ecstatic engagement with nature.
Engagement of your spirit and physical movement through the landscape can be combined in a number of ways. Here are some examples:
- Flowing with the river. Run/walk along the bank of a creek or river in the direction of flow (in a downstream direction). Allow the river to energize you. Flow with the river. I was hiking along the Potomac River on the Billy Goat Trail when I felt that I was the river for the first time, without having to think about it and without having the analytical mind engaged.
- Running with or after animals and letting your heart race. We can also play the roles of (or channel) animals while trance dancing or at any time in our daily lives.
- Dancing with trees. I enjoy moving among the trees in forests or parks. Sometimes I sing to an aspect of the Green Man who dances around trees. I have enjoyed doing the Tsalagi Dance in front of the Music School of Indiana

University where the postures of sycamore trees give the appearance that the trees are dancing.

Before ecstatically engaging with nature entities, or before working with any of the techniques that are described in this book, it is ethical to get permission as a baseline as well as seek synergy and mutual benefit.

T10.12. Elemental connection.
Bathe in the Sun. Delve into the mud, sand, gravel, and soil. Immerse in water. Feel air in the lungs and on the face. Feel the substances that make up the Earth.

One of my favorite elemental connection exercises was a group exercise in which we coated each other with mud, baked in the Sun, and then swam in a pond to wash the mud away. It was nourishing and cathartic and these feelings were amplified because it was a group exercise. We encouraged each other's bliss.

We are connecting just by being in nature for even just a few minutes, with or without consciously working with techniques. Imagine the effect that comes from spending hours, days, months, or years in immersion. Being immersed in the wild daily for months (especially if camping) can produce a deep plugged-in state and enhance base level spirit awareness (see Chapter 11 for comments about spending long periods out in nature).

T10.13. Spend time immersed in the wilderness!!!
WILDERNESS brings nature immersion to a new level. Another level of getting "plugged in" is possible. Wilderness is raw, mystical, and powerfully beautiful. We can feel the raw power as well as embody our primal nature when we are there, and essences and energies of wilderness can remain precious to us when we are not there. For some folks, wilderness has a special place in the heart and for others it is the only reason the heart beats. Being in wilderness (of varying degrees) creates a transformation in our consciousness which allows us to connect more deeply and forget our false sense of separateness. The otherworldly nature of wilderness can shock you into being fully present. In the wilderness, you have to work hard not to get into the moment; finding a meditative trance is easy.

> **Transformation**
> Walk down a suburban road
> Turn onto a path
> Disappear into the woods
> Then stray from the path
> Booted feet shuffle the leaves of the forest floor
> Wind penetrates L. L. Bean clothing
> Cool and harsh against the skin
> With mild hunger or boredom
> Nibble on a handful of trail mix
> A swig of bottled water
>
> As squirrels chatter and cardinals flit about

Thoughts of work dissipate
Anxieties of the "rat race" mellow
Insecure voices in the head quiet down

Notice the movement out of the corner of the eye
Hear the ground vibrate and sticks break
Heart beating with the gallop of the stag
Give chase!!

Hiking boots clomp on sticks and dead leaves
Urgency pulsing in the head
Running
Over ridge and hollow
Following the stag

Beginning to use hands and feet
Tossing aside the backpack and clothing
Running with greater speed
Mouth watering for venison
Hair sprouts on belly and face
And quivers with the excitement of the hunt
Running
Kick off the boots
Running
Shed the remaining clothing
Running
On hairy feet and hands
Running

Paws barely touch the forest floor
Moving among oaks, tulip poplars, and hickories
Air flows through the fur coat
Feel the wind in the eyes
And upon the snout
Tongue aching
Anticipating the stag's blood

Leap through the crisp air
Sink big sharp teeth into bloody flesh
Tearing into muscle – warm from the chase
Tasting hot blood
Rip out the heart
And swallow the stag's essence
Consuming the spirit
Feel the flow
Vitality and strength

Hunger fulfilled
Desire quenched
Saunter to the ridge top

Tilting head back …
Arrggghoooooooooooooooooowwwwwwwwwwghhh

Adam Davis, 12/22/2000

CHAPTER 11. Extended vigils and multi-day deepening.

A diverse mix of spiritual nourishment comes from being in a wilderness place for an extended period of time without keeping busy, working on specific tasks, or emotional escapes.

Participants in vision quests and vigils of various traditions have reported being visited by spirit animals. I have not experienced this during my vigils, even though I have connected with animals in other ceremonies and through shamanic journeys. My vigils contained anti-visions and anti-epiphanies. They cut away the distractions and surficial concerns and showed me essences and inner workings. I got more of a look at my core and at the fabric of existence than I did receive omens or feel particular spirits during the vigils. This sitting with the essential energies occurs for a number of people who undertake the ordeals of vigils.

Three rites of passage vigils conducted during different phases of my life were similar in some fundamental ways. I had formal dialogue with aspects of the land, including through prayers and offerings beforehand and as the vigils progressed. I was committed to being open to guidance from nature spirits as well as any archetypal energies that blessed me with their presence. They encouraged me to deepen my relationship with the vigil location and myself. Although I felt I was connecting with land and self on multiple levels, I have the impression that much of the land connection was subconscious, especially during the middle of the experience. The wilderness was a backdrop for my personal work. I felt the land strongly and consciously at times, including otherworldly aspects of the land, and at other times I was focused on thoughts and emotions generated by internal personal work and not consciously sensing nature.

These vigils also differed from one another. The trial of being with myself varied in intensity among the three vigils. I was in different emotional states each time, and each emotional state influenced vigil challenges. In some cases, I worked with fire. I also went fire-free. At Lake Monroe, I felt most energized and "plugged in" during the preparation for the vigil. On Half Moon Mountain, each part of the experience was thick, I had several hours of intense discomfort, and I connected with several pine trees that were growing in the thin ridgetop soil. On Pickerel Lake in Minnesota, I was very "in the moment" and spent much time communing with mosquitos and flies. After two of my vigils, I was welcomed back by a group. I enjoyed the feeling of being part of a rich spiritual community. I was not greeted after a vigil on Half Moon Mountain, which was beneficial in a different way. The personal vigil work seemed to continue during my drive back home and during my transition back into my home life.

I have had similar experiences while participating in group vigils on the Winter Solstice. We carried on the tradition of lighting and tending a fire all night to ensure the safe return of the Sun. Solo multi-day backpacking trips have had a similar feel to the "alone with the multiverse" aspect of the intentional vigil experiences.

Vision quests are important rites of passage and journeys for guidance in Native

American traditions. See Wolf Moondance (2004) for some tips that are useful in preparing for a vision quest including prayer sticks and ties as well as ideas for prayers.

In a similar vein as vision quests, vigils have been rites of passage in Druid groves (groups). Also bearing some similarities are the multi-day solo experiences common to survival skills classes and wilderness journeys such as multi-week canoe trips in the Boundary Waters of Minnesota (Voyageur Outward Bound School, 2013). The multi-month experience of backpacking the entire length of a long trail (e.g., Appalachian Trail, Pacific Crest Trail, Tuscarora Trail, or North Country Trail) has transformed the lives of diverse folks.

I advocate getting advice from elders or mentors as well as spirit guides before engaging in vision quests or other intense solo experiences, traditional or otherwise.

CHAPTER 12. Omens, metaphors, symbols.

"We are the rocks dancing" John Seed

Replete with multiple dimensions of meaning and layers upon layers of symbology, nature gifts us with inspirations and messages in many forms.

Inspirational metaphors

Characteristics and behaviors of animals are used in sayings, as symbols to rally around, and as tools in a variety of situations. "Quiet as a mouse", "free as a bird", "eyes of a hawk", "strong as a bull", and "busy as a beaver" are all sayings that highlight or romanticize our behavior in relation to behaviors of animals. The skunk reminds me to do my own thing and to protect myself from those that would interfere. The bear symbolizes resourcefulness for me. In some traditions, bear is a symbol of healing and transformation as well as a shamanic guide.

Trees that can live in thin or no soil can be very inspiring: pine trees growing on a sandstone cliff in the central Appalachians, oaks and eastern red cedar trees growing in thin soils above sandstones in southern Indiana, birch trees growing in fractures in metamorphic rock in New England, and others. Birches are symbolic of new beginnings as they are quick to colonize disturbed areas. They can send their roots for long distances along the surface to find a good place to go down into the soil, which reminds me to travel miles to seek nourishment.

Figure 12.1. Roots of a black birch (*Betula lenta*) along Amethyst Brook in Amherst, MA.

Nature reminds us of cycles of growth and decay, and of death and rebirth. We see leaves emerge during the spring season and grow, and later we see them dry up and fall. We see living things growing from the decomposed remnants of previous generations. American chestnut sprouts come up from the root systems of the large trees that were once a prominent part of Appalachian forests. New life comes up from previous roots. Young trees try to grow tall, again and again, despite being attacked by a foreign invasive species. You can observe a dead tree, a dying sapling (falling prey to the chestnut blight), and newer shoots attached to the same old roots. They are symbols of multiple generations, longevity, and life from death. A mountain in North Carolina was named "Generations Mountain" in honor of the American chestnut.

Figure 12.2. American chestnut (*Castanea dentata*) shoots, sprouting from the same old roots as multiple past chestnut saplings (such as the small dead trunk in the center of the photo).

Swollen buds on trees in early spring remind me of potential and fullness before action. Emergence of leaves and flowers from buds inspires me to awaken and grow. The emergence of a root and stem from a seed is similarly inspiring.

Figure 12.3. Emergence of spring. a) Northern red oak sprouting leaves in Vincennes, IN. b) Fiddleheads in Northampton, MA. c) Swollen bitternut hickory bud, preparing to put forth leaves. d) Root and shoot have come out of an acorn.

Blooming of flowers in the spring is another treasure. I make a point of seeking the flowers out when they bloom. They are a source of joy for me. A hillside of trout lilies along the Mill River in Northampton, MA, generated an upwelling of joy.

Figure 12.4. Trout lilies on the side slope of the Mill River Valley in Northampton, MA, on April 26, 2013.

Wildflowers are also a source of happiness throughout the summer and fall as new species begin to bloom while the flowers of others are withering and transforming to fruit. I look forward to *Eupatorium rugosum* and *Aster lateriflorus* in the fall as much as a second wave of spring wildflowers that might include *Trillium recurvatum* and *Packera aurea*. When walking my regular trails, I look for who is getting ready to flower, who is blooming, and who is fruiting.

I have loved meeting wildflowers during my continental and intercontinental travels: desert wildflowers, wildflowers of the Scottish Highlands, North Woods wildflowers, and others. Wildflower occurrence factors into my travel plans. I have enjoyed getting to New England lowlands early in the spring season to catch the first skunk cabbage blooms, I have visited north facing slopes with limestone bedrock to see a rich diversity of wildflowers (including rare ones), and I have prioritized hiking and backpacking in early June in the Appalachians so that I can see the slopes covered with mountain laurel blossoms.

Figure 12.5. White flowers of mountain laurel blooming in the Holyoke Range, MA.

Many hours spent getting to know a diversity of wildflowers has been a large developmental influence, inspiring me to open my joy channel so that I may blossom and move into a period of inspired activity and production.

The power of flowing creeks and rivers, and the dynamic nature of channels are excellent sources of inspiration. Riffles and pools as well as the tendency of creeks to meander instill within me a sense of awe. They remind me of the ethic of constantly seeking and discerning the course. Confluences of two rivers or creeks, regional drainage patterns (e.g., dendritic, trellis, or rectangular), and channel types (e.g., braided, meandering, or straight) all inspire certain qualities and link to metaphysical properties. Flowing with the Potomac River while hiking the Billy Goat Trail was a breakthrough for me – one of the first times I was the flowing river as opposed to observing the flowing river. One of my more memorable and powerful shamanic journeys involved tumbling down the White River. The blood flow in my veins is the flow of rivers, streams, and groundwater.

"Natural wells and pools and running streams, even large lakes, are gateways for the Otherworld Powers" Ian Corrigan

I feel a connection with my ancestors at the ocean. This may be a blood memory of my European ancestors or could be a very old memory of early life evolving in the oceans before colonizing land. The immensity and abyssal quality of the ocean puts me in touch with the great mystery. Oceans are both powerful shapers of the land along the coastlines and powerful drivers of regional and global climate.

Various birds have power for me. The bravery of chickadees was the talk of my house when I was a kid – they stood up to the bullies at the bird feeder. Vultures have a particular mystique (an air of foreboding), and seeing 10 or more of them on a tree without leaves is an impressive site. Seeing eagles awakens my sense of freedom and leaves me in awe of true majesty. Seeing one glide overhead along Lake Monroe picked me up toward a higher self.

Certain regions have inspirational and other powers. For example, I have felt an uplifting of spirit when spending time in the Appalachians. While driving through the NC and VA Appalachians in August of 2012, I felt a much needed healing occur inside me. I am grateful for this instance and other regional healing effects. I am grateful for diverse land energies that have supported healing, inspiration, catharsis, renewal, cleansing, and other kinds of transformation. The ways that we are personally inspired and nurtured relate to the sacredness and specific powers of places within the landscape.

T12.1. Remember and discover aspects of nature that inspire you.
I invite you to take some time to reflect upon joys and other emotions that you have experienced in conjunction with being inspired by a natural process or behavior in the past. In the present, you can observe your feelings in response to different beings or aspects of nature. Are you inspired by the song of a particular bird? Do you take note and feel enlivened by the presence of a tree that you pass on a walk? You can open up and begin to discover which aspects of nature really speak to you.

Based on inspirational qualities, we can choose nature materials, symbols, and images to wear, carry, or use to decorate our homes. My life has been influenced by the type of tree that my ceremonial staff came from and how it has changed through time. My first staff was silver maple, which gave way to hickory, which was replaced by red maple, which was followed by black walnut. The staff of silver maple accompanied me during a quick germination and rapid growth stage of my life. I took heart in a staff of hickory, a symbol of my toughness and ability to persevere during my dissertation years. The red maple staff was both a gift from a red maple tree and a gift from a friend. Red maple fit my life circumstances at that time, and the staff being a gift from a friend also fit. The black walnut staff (which ended its tour of duty in 2022) was supportive of cleansing, plugging in, discernment, and taking my work to new levels. In addition to carrying a staff, I have carried other nature beings with me during my travels. I have carried a bear claw and garnets for protection and strength, an amethyst to promote awareness and vision, and other nature beings for specific effects.

Spirit animals, patrons, and guides

Aspects of nature can be engaged in deeply spiritual and religious ways. In some traditional Native American cultures and in enclaves of modern North American culture, people choose to elevate (or mark as extra special) the relationship with one animal – making it a "spirit animal". In some cases, this is an animal that the human personally identifies with. Threads of behavior may be shared between human and animal. Knowledge of a spirit animal usually comes through a special omen or some other divine experience. Spirit animals are said to choose humans by visiting during a multi-day vision quest. Wolf and bear are popular spirit animals, while mosquito is not as common. Animals are also associated with signs of the Zoroastrian zodiac (e.g., Pisces – fish, Scorpio – scorpion and eagle, Leo – lion, Capricorn – goat, Taurus – bull, Cancer – crab, and Aries – ram). The "Shadows of the Apt" series of novels by Tchaikovsky is set in a world in which the races of people have characteristics linked to particular insects. In this world, moth people can fly and prefer nighttime while ant people can communicate through a group mind. An animal, or plant, associated with a tribe, lineage, or tradition is considered a "totem". The term totem sometimes gets used for the individual, a "personal totem", and can sometimes be conflated with the term "spirit animal".

Another related practice involves working with "patrons" and "matrons", engaging in personal mentor or devotional relationships with particular entities of nature (the terms patron and matron can also apply to relationships with deities or saints). I have worked with a patron mountain (Half Moon Mountain in West Virginia, USA), and I also have had a patron tree (hickory – *Carya*) who has helped me persevere.

Trees, landforms, animals, and other nature entities (whether considered patron, spirit animal, or otherwise) can provide inspiration based on their physical and metaphysical properties. Here are some properties and kinds of medicine associated with several nature entities:

- Skunk – Protection. Desire to be left alone to do your own thing. Earth and soil. Communicating boundaries. Vitality is associated with the white stripe (Andrews, 1993). Skunks associate with other skunks.
- Black bear – Protection, resourcefulness, healing, and ability to look within for answers (Andrews, 1993). See Gore (1995) for an effective standing bear healing posture that I have found to be a good way to learn about bear medicine. A bear spirit animal can provide insight and discernment to help you express and possibly defend your truth in life (Steiger, 1997).
- Wolf – Investment in social hierarchies and keen senses (especially smell) (Andrews, 1993). Teaches us about community. Emblem of Christian Saints: Francis of Assisi, Edmund of East Anglia, and Wolfgang (Steiger, 1997). Some indigenous peoples of North America had clans, societies, and dances that revered the sacredness of the wolf (Lake-Thom, 1997).
- Frog – Underworld. Transformation. A symbol of rebirth and fertility, and associated with the goddess Hecate (Steiger, 1997). The frog posture in Gore (1995) has been cathartic for me.
- River – Flow of different types. Life giving. Carrying things away.
- Fly – Larva are involved in the decay of mammal flesh. An agent of transformation. Hearing from a fly at a Council of All Beings (see Chapter 21) was a much needed reminder of the importance of insects to ecosystems.
- Garnet, staurolite schist – Transformation, new growth, alignment.
- Red winged blackbird – Wetlands and fields near water, energy cycling with the seasons (Andrews, 1993).

Figure 12.6. Red winged blackbird perched at the top of an alder tree in a wetland at the western end of Fitzgerald Lake, MA.

Additional metaphysical properties of rocks, trees, and animals that can inform our relationships with aspects of nature are explored through discussions of techniques and other stories in various locations throughout the book.

We may have relationships with several aspects of nature and can choose to work with them as divine entities. In recognition of these multiple relationships, some traditions and individuals work with the concept of guiding spirits (and saints and angels in Christian traditions) which involves working with multiple "guides" rather than, or in addition to, one dominant patron or spirit animal (e.g., folks work with multiple spirit animals, multiple nature spirits, multiple saints, and/or multiple deities). Some think of the spirit world as a hierarchy of tiers of spirits (e.g., deities being at the top of the pyramid and fairies lower down), while others focus on the character of individual guides without worrying much about categories.

We can have devotional, theological, and/or inspirational relationships with as many nature beings as are willing to work with us. Many people work with Mother Earth or Grandmother Earth, and many work with a Sky Father as well. Sun deities and river goddesses are staples of modern religious beliefs as well as beliefs of antiquity. Spirits of certain animals or landforms are also featured in multiple belief systems. Some believe that the spirits choose us rather than the other way around. Others believe the relationship involves choice on both sides. Deities and spirits from multiple traditions are discussed in Chapter 17.

Working with others can provide very fertile discussions about inspirational, magical, spirit animal, guiding spirit, and other kinds of relationships. During a sharing portion of a workshop, a woman asked me about eagles. It motivated me to relive some experiences, do some research, and get back to her. In honor of her question, I share some aspects of eagle medicine:

- MAJESTY, POWER, and FREEDOM. While in Minnesota in late May, 2012, I walked along the Mississippi River and saw several bald eagles flying and soaring in the sky. The omen for me at that time was freedom – specifically a message to let myself be free to explore some of my rich opportunities, instead of binding myself with my fears. The majesty and power of the eagle has impressed me every time that I have seen one.
- DEITIES. The eagle is associated with Llew (Jones and Jones, 1993) and Zeus, and is a divine messenger in the Vedic tradition (Steiger, 1997). There is also an ancient Tibetan eagle deity named Khyung (Mythical Creatures List, 2013). Indigenous peoples have worked with eagle deities and revered eagles among birds. Some folks work with the Aztec goddess "Cihuacoatl" as Eagle Woman (Goddesses, 2010). In the late 1990s, I attended a ritual that featured Lady Liberty (Bonewits). It linked a North American sovereignty goddess with the eagle in a way that resonated well with me. The eagle was also a symbol of the sovereignty of roman emperors (Steiger, 1997). Some versions of a traditional chant link eagles to a father deity and other versions link eagles to the Earth Mother:

  > Mother I feel you under my feet
  > Mother I hear your heartbeat
  > Mother I see your eagles fly
  > Spirit take me higher.

- EAGLE WING. In the Tsalagi Dance of Life, the eagle is symbolic of the masculine energy that is expended to initiate the dance (Waterhawk, 2002).
- MIDDLE EARTH. The relationship of eagles, land, and magician in the Lord of the Rings Trilogy resonates well with me (Tolkien, 1954). This relationship is reminiscent of the Earth Dragon.
- EAGLE AS A SPIRIT ANIMAL OF EAST. On Beltane (Mayday) 2013, an eagle took flight from the east toward and over our sacred site, letting us know that it was time to start the ceremony. It was time to honor the directions, starting in the east. An eagle is considered to be an omen that indicates a good ceremony with a good group of people (Lake-Thom, 1997).

Omens and signs

Sometimes there is an auspicious synchronicity or a sixth sense involved as we turn to look just in time to see a sight that is rare and/or directly relevant to some aspect of our life. One of these situations occurred to me at Fitzgerald Lake in western Massachusetts. I was walking along the trail, absorbed in my thoughts and looking down at the ground, when something caused me to look to the left and up just in time to see an absolute gem – a large barred owl perched in a small understory tree pivoting his or her head. In a similar instance, I saw a green man in a shrub outside a club in Hartford, CT, when I was at an emotional low and in a vulnerable situation. I had the impression that he was watching over me and there to support me. Sometimes people see cultural symbols of note appearing in nature such as in rock fractures, sand and gravel patterns in the bed of a stream, or lines in a tree's bark. I also sometimes see shapes in the clouds that indicate energy patterns. I call these types of occurrences omens when they are screaming for me to pay attention so that they can highlight important energy patterns. All natural phenomena that have messages for us can be considered omens.

T12.2. Appearance of wildlife as omens.
Folks consider the timely appearance of rare, beautiful, and/or auspicious wildlife to be omens. Examples include a vulture soaring overhead, the call of a crow, the wail of a loon, a bear in the underbrush, and a black snake on a rock. Postures of plants and bird speech can be omens and are part of the collective dialogue with the land that is occurring whether we are aware of it or not. In addition, since the mundane is the sacred, the first dandelion to bloom in the yard can be an omen.

Connecting with nature can involve pain and unpleasant emotions which can be messages, omens, or symbolic in other ways. Bee stings, allergic reactions, spider bites, and fears have caused me to see places in different ways. On multiple occasions, the timing of spider bites has told me to pay closer attention to nature.

Divination

We can deliberately allow omens to emerge. Basically, the process involves opening to energy patterns and letting inspiration come into the consciousness. We can use formal systems or methods to help us see the energy patterns and interpret events in a cosmological sense. The process of "divining" (learning and interpreting) these patterns is called divination. "Seeking an omen" is a way that divination is done in a targeted way [e.g., in the core order of Ár nDraíocht Féin ritual (Ár nDraíocht Féin, 2013)], and may involve formal systems of methods and dogma.

T12.3. Nature scrying.
Intentionally looking and letting aspects of nature speak to us is a way to gain divine insight. This process is sometimes called scrying and commonly involves looking into a pool of water or fire (or special ritual tools like mirrors or crystal balls). I enjoy sitting and going into a trance with a soft focus on one place in nature (I could be looking at one patch of a forest floor, looking at the surrounding area, or otherwise guiding my awareness). While in this light trance, I allow information to come to me with all my senses – I allow the omen to emerge.

Sets of symbols (e.g., oghams, rune futharks, rocks and minerals, cards with nature images upon them, and mixtures of nature objects) can be used to receive omens from nature, possibly because the symbol sets are based upon observable properties of nature elements, they symbolize aspects of nature, or both.

The term ogham refers to symbols used for communication by the Celts, and the term also refers to individual groups of these symbols. The Tree Ogham is the best known ogham, and is the most widely used for divination (Ellison, 2007). In the Tree

Ogham, the symbols correspond to European plant species, although some North Americans rely on closely related North American species to carry similar meanings. My personal ogham set includes staves made from North American trees that are close relatives of the European ogham species (most having the same genus) and a few European species. When creating my initial set of 20 symbols, I talked with many trees before accepting gifts of small staves, from the ground or dead lower branches, that would eventually be included. This process was approximately 2 years in duration. Over 10 years later, I added 5 extra symbols and a full second set of the 25 symbols of the Tree Ogham (also acquired through conversations with many trees). To use the Tree Ogham in divination, I draw staves from a bag knitted especially for the purpose of carrying them. I attempt to ascertain what the staves are telling me based on traditional meanings, the dialogue I am having with them, and the place and circumstances of the reading. For traditional meanings to recall during readings, as well as for pre-reading and post-reading study, I have consulted Ellison (2007), Nathair Bheag (1998), and Mac Coitir (2003). The correspondence tables of Mac Coitir (2003) are well constructed. Here are example traditional and situational meanings (from study and experience) for some of the Tree Ogham:

- Dair. English oak (I have both bur oak and northern red oak in my double set). Represents strength. The guardian oak. Strong oak doors.
- Nion (Nin). This symbol links to the ash in the correspondences of Ellison (2007); Mac Coitir (2003) indicates that while ash was the tree associated with this ogham character during medieval times, cherry is the correct correspondence.
- Luis. European mountain ash (my set includes a stave from a European mountain ash that escaped from cultivation near my childhood home). Also known as the rowan. Symbolizes protection. This tree is found circling sacred sites in Europe.
- Saille. Willow. Flow. Lowlands and associated properties. Flexibility. Darker mysteries. I obtained my first Saille stave from a willow growing along a small stream that flows through the Bloomington campus of Indiana University.
- Tinne. Holly. My set includes American holly from the Chesapeake region as well as non-native holly from Northampton, MA. Drawing Tinne during divination can introduce a marshal character to the omen as Tinne is associated with fire, reckoning, and justice.
- Huath. Hawthorn. Protection. Thorns. Terror. Formidable. The bite of the wilds. The bite at the edges of the wild. Barrier. One of nature's reminders to ask permission and be respectful. A thorn in the hand of my brother as he busts through a hawthorn thicket. Heart medicine.
- Beith. European white birch. My set includes a river birch (*Betula nigra*) stave. New beginnings. Resourcefulness.
- Ailm. Fir. Pine and spruce both serve as Ailm in my set. Symbolizes far sight and vision of the future. It is the "ahhhh" associated with discovery.
- Eadhadh. Aspen. I collected an Eadhadh stave from an aspen felled during a logging operation in Morgan-Monroe State Forest in southern Indiana. The waving leaf of the aspen has been associated with friendship and communication (Ellison, 2007).

See Ellison (2007) for descriptions and divinatory meanings of the whole set of the Tree Ogham, and Mac Coitir (2003) for a different take on the correspondences and meanings. Figure 12.7 shows ogham staves used for divination.

Figure 12.7. Photograph of an ogham cast – a method of divination that uses the Tree Ogham.

Some of the symbols known as runes also link to nature. The Elder Futhark rune "Ingwaz" is associated with a fertility god, "Hagalaz" refers to "hail" and represents nature's wrath, "Laguz" is linked to wet areas and water, "Sowelo" represents the Sun, "Dagaz" represents dawn or a breakthrough, and "Jera" represents the harvest and year (Paxson, 2005).

Using runes in divination can involve pulling discs that are marked with rune symbols from a bag, and it can also be done by tossing (casting) marked objects or unmarked sticks. Here are some example casting methods:

- Small sticks can be thrown up in the air so that they land in a pile, and then the seer can look within the pile to see which runes emerge.
- Discs or squares with runes carved in them can also be tossed into the air, and the spatial pattern in which specific runes land can provide context for the reading. When using this method, a number of seers read with the discs or squares that land face up (i.e., with rune symbol visible) and remove those that land face down.
- Sticks with runes carved in or painted on them can be used for a casting. In a

rune cast done with this method, each stick carries the meanings of a rune, and additional runes can be formed by the way the sticks intersect each other. The rune of each stick, runes formed by the way multiple of the sticks fit together, the spatial distribution of these runes, and other situational dynamics can all contribute to the reading (Sibley, 2009).

Also, runes observed among our surroundings can provide omens. In August of 2012, I saw the runes Dagaz, Mannaz, Wunjo, and Gebo in basalt joints (fractures) in the Holyoke Range along the border of the Massachusetts towns of Holyoke and Easthampton. These runes told of the potential for a joyful new beginning received as a gift through self mastery. In another rune story, I found a necklace in a thrift store in Vincennes, IN, that featured a Dagaz pendant. The next day, as I drove through the Green County hills at dawn, I had a breakthrough regarding my dissertation after many months of spinning my wheels. I considered Dagaz to be an omen of the breakthrough.

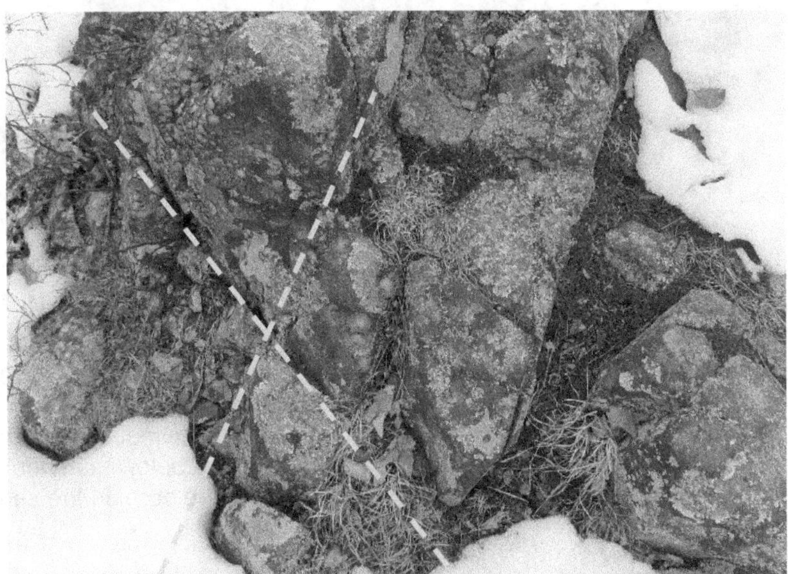

Figure 12.8. Photograph of an outcrop of fractured basalt bedrock of the Holyoke Range. The rune Gebo is indicated with dashed lines. What runes do you see?

Both runes and ogham get used for other magical purposes. They are frequently used as charms, talismans, and words of power. They are inscribed on staves, pendants, and rings as well as tattooed on bodies. Runes get used in ceremonies for establishing sacred space, they get used in healing, and they get used in other kinds of transformational work. My mission, confirmed and realized through a series of ceremonies and personal work, is symbolized through a personal symbol and has a phrase written in ogham to go with it: "service to land and people".

Divination can also be done using rocks and minerals. Figure 12.9 is a photograph of the results of drawing from a bag of rocks and minerals six different times. Potassium feldspar and granite (the two in the center of Figure 12.9) indicate strength and stability. The dark, dioritic rock at the bottom of the photograph could indicate mixed emotions or primal energies. Calcite (top of Figure 12.9) can indicate soft, tranquil healing. The ignimbrite on the left and the schist on the right indicate alignment and transformation in response to pressures or stresses.

Figure 12.9. Rocks and minerals drawn from a rock and mineral divination set. This reading is a cosmological map and a map of the self: core, primal influence below; soft nourishment on the surface; and responses to transformation on either side of the core, in the sequence of change.

There are many other methods of divination. During the "seek an omen" portion of a Black Bear Grove ceremony, the omen was interpreted based on the release of an owl and what the owl did after being released. During another such ceremony, an omen was received through a period of inspired speech by the participants, termed a "Quaker style" omen by one of the participants, referring to the "speak when moved" aspect of Friends meetings.

To help with the interpretation of an omen, I make note of what I was thinking when the sign came. I also note parallel messages or omens that relate. At times, I have experienced what I call "pile on omens" that consist of many omens occurring in a short period of time that all point to a similar message. During some periods of my life, I have received "nag omens" that are repetitions of the same message over longer periods of time. Sometimes I have incorporated the information into my decision making process and other times I have not.

Correspondences (linkages between nature aspects and meanings) can be used in the seeking of an omen (divination) and can help with the interpretation of emergent omens. They can also help us optimize the use and power of nature metaphors. We can use correspondences to harness the power of nature to encourage certain patterns to come into or leave our lives. Correspondences are useful when choosing and working with a spirit animal or patron, picking talismans, exploring metaphorical inspiration, composing prayers, choosing offerings for aspects of nature, and interpreting information from shamanic journeys. They may also help with investigating and understanding power spots or energy conduits in the landscape.

Aspects of nature can have power for us through the law of association in magic (Bonewits, 1971). Basically, an entity or energy that is being used in a magical working has power because one or more of its properties corresponds to qualities that the magic wishes to encourage or promote. This principle is useful when attempting to incorporate specific objects or nature beings in magical workings. For example, a particular gemstone that is very strong and hard and cannot be broken can be used as a symbol for bonds that are everlasting (e.g., diamonds on wedding rings).

Physical and metaphysical properties of animals, plants, rocks, minerals, hot springs, and other aspects of nature have been described and passed down through folklore and tradition. One of the earliest written summaries of folklore correspondences of rocks, minerals, plants, and other aspects of nature is Pliny's "Natural History" (Pliny, 77-150/1956). The written tradition continues in modern times with works such as the rock and gem book of Cunningham (1988).

There are a diversity of properties associated with natural essences. Correspondences are modified and/or new ones created by each person who works with nature's gifts for healing or magical purposes.

T12.4. Work with plants, rocks, and minerals for healing.
Raw or cooked plants; infusions (e.g., teas) of dried plants; tinctures of herbs; homeopathic amplifications of herbal extracts; essences of rocks and minerals; placements of plants, rocks, or crystals in home or office; and placements of crystals on chakras during sound therapies are all used in healing and other kinds of transformation. Herbal concoctions continue to gain popularity and multiple aisles of them are available for purchase in health food and New Age stores. Although, from a connecting with the land perspective, it is more instructive to collect and prepare them yourself. If you are thinking about embarking down an herbalist path or increasing the amount of these remedies that you use, I suggest learning from herbalists of good repute and establishing plans for doing it safely.

Many plants have healing properties, and there are a variety of references and practitioners with information about them. Brown (1985) is a well reputed reference that provides healing properties of plants that can be collected in natural areas in North America. Another reference, Hoffmann (1996), includes correspondences as well as practical guidelines for making and using herbal remedies. Hoffmann (1996) also contains some helpful tips for navigating the vast sea of herbal references. Raw plant tissue, essential oils, and tinctures from various plants are used to support or encourage health or changes in circumstances. Advice regarding the use of concentrated or other processed versions of plant essences is beyond the scope of this book, but worthwhile to delve into if it fits your calling and circumstances.

Rocks and minerals in various forms are used for magical purposes. Pendants and other jewelry with gemstones are worn as charms. These may contain gems associated with zodiac signs (birthstones) or that have specific magical uses such as protection, healing, or strength. Whole crystals are used in healing work, including chakra cleansing and balancing. This work is multifaceted (like many crystals) and there is much knowledge to explore. Melody (1995) and Cunningham (1988) are popular collections of healing and other magical properties associated with minerals and rocks. Cunningham (1988) describes his sources through an annotated bibliography, making this book a good jumping off point into the sea of rock, mineral, and crystal magic literature. The correspondences and healing techniques mentioned in Elsbeth (1998) seem to have Native American influence.

There are many different sets of correspondences (SOCs) used in the work described in this chapter. Reasons for the many sets include the many traits of nature entities and energies, the existence of diverse cultural traditions (see Chapter 17 for legends and stories associated with animals, plants, rocks, minerals, and specific landforms), and the diversity of human minds producing many different opinions. The meanings discussed above for use in ogham and rune divination, herbals, and rock and mineral magic references are examples of SOCs. For more examples of SOCs, see the correspondence tables in the back of Crowley (1977), Mac Coitir (2003), Wolf Moondance (2004), Cunningham (1988), and the inspiration and spirit animal discussions earlier in this chapter. One of these or other published SOCs may work well for you. Alternatively you can create your own YAFSOC (Yet Another Functional Set Of Correspondences). The linkage between chapters of this book and specific nature beings indicated in the Table of Contents is a YAFSOC that was set up to provide another lens for viewing the book topics and an additional framework by which the reader can navigate the book. Sets of correspondences can link into one another, so perhaps your YAFSOC could be a personal set of guidelines that helps you pick existing SOCs for specific purposes.

There are many schools of thought regarding the application of metaphysical knowledge. Some practitioners are conservative when using a plant or stone for healing, while others may throw caution to the wind and do things like placing crystals directly on the chakras and ringing crystal bowls for hours. When starting to work with a new modality, I sometimes decide to err on the side of caution.

CHAPTER 13. Working with trees.

"Every posture of every tree branch is an omen" Jerry Nees

People have benefited from gifts and commodities taken from trees for much of their lives. Trees have helped us shelter from the Sun and storm, read books, and clean our bodies. Many of us have slightly more romantic notions of our relationships to trees as well. One of my favorite mentoring moments came during a story about a tree. A Naturalist mentor told me the story of a young hickory tree. He told of a young, slow growing hickory extending its trunk up toward the Sun. As time progressed, faster growing trees shaded the hickory. In response, the hickory put out a side branch to seek sunlight in a different direction and let its vertical trunk die back. Repeating this process over and over made the hickory wood knotty and tough. The story inspires me to be tough and perseverant in my life.

We can be intentional about how we work with these beautiful creatures, including showing them proper respect. Developing relationships with trees can involve the specific application of individual or combinations of techniques mentioned in other chapters. We may see and talk with spirits within trees, connect with the energy or aura of a tree as a whole, connect through emotions that trees inspire within us, and/or marvel at the natural wonder of these creatures. Many people have personal relationships with trees, which may manifest as an ongoing regular dialogue with one or more trees. Some see faces or other beings in or on trees, and some are able to see tree auras.

T13.1. Scan for synergies.
Sensing what degrees and types of interactions are desired by the trees (or other nature beings) and ourselves is central to being respectful and reverent. This kind of sensing can be simplified to "what feels right", which can involve how the body responds to energies that are present as well as messages received when asking about what kind of synergy is present.

T13.2. Walk around a tree.
Walk sunwise (clockwise) around a tree and focus on the breathing. I suggest doing at least 3 revolutions to ensure that you deepen into this activity, and more is better. If you are open but not analyzing while doing this, impressions can come from the tree to you. They may show up as images in your third eye (on the inside of your forehead). Thoughts could pop into or emerge in your head. The tree may be talking to you, and you can listen.

T13.3. Tree visualization.
Visualize yourself as a tree and journey down through the soil by putting out roots and up into the sky by extending your branches upward and outward. This is a popular variety of two powers visualization, an example of which was given in Chapter 7, because the downward and upward growth of trees can serve as inspiration and a guide for the use of Basic Visualization Technique (BVT).

T13.4. Go into a tree and look out.
A more active exercise involves visualizing your essence or consciousness moving into a specific tree (make sure you ask for permission before going in, and be prepared for a no answer). You can move up the xylem (vascular tissue for moving nutrients) of the tree and then look at the world from the tree's point of view. One can deepen into this exercise in a very meditative way, and can employ creative perspective shifts to begin to empathize with how the tree might view the outside world, how it may perceive current events and sense energy patterns, and what it might remember. I vividly remember the power of the perspective shift during my first exposure to this technique in a workshop by Skip Ellison in Prince William Forest Park, VA. Emptiness meditation and shamanic journeys are good ways to prepare for this type of exercise. While preparing to facilitate or participate in this exercise in a group setting, it can be very rewarding to brainstorm and discuss possibilities for enriching the experience.

T13.5. Visualize your place on the World Tree.

T13.6. Honor trees.
There are many ways to honor trees. There are many ways to show them respect and give them praise in your personal practice or within group activities. Here are some ways that trees can be honored:
- Bowing.
- Sharing intentions.
- Respecting, and attempting to provide, what a tree communicates that it wants.
- Gathering around a tree in a circle.
- Giving energy to a tree, grove, or forest. This could include giving a tree a hug or Reiki.
- Toasts.
- An honoring speech or song for a tree or trees.
- Physical offerings.
- Giving thanks.
- Service.

The southern Indiana Druid group called "Black Bear Grove" has worked with a variety of methods to do the ceremonial honoring of a Sacred Center (Well, Fire, and Tree). This work has included gathering at a tree and singing to it, touching it, smiling with it, dancing with it, and more.

T13.7. Invoke trees in ceremony.
One way to work with trees in ceremony is to invoke them as guardians and/or protectors. One time, I almost drove by the turn off for a ceremony site in Massachusetts because an oak branch had fallen down onto the roadway from the tree located at the fork in the road – I had met the guardian oak. I got out and stated my purpose and good will and then listened. I also left a physical offering before moving on to the ceremony.

A large white oak, growing near Allen's Creek in southern Indiana, was invoked as the guardian during a Druid ceremony, because it seemed to watch over the whole valley. In other cases, a particular tree seems to guard the pathway into sacred sites. Trees may play the guardian role day in and day out in various places within the landscape continuously for years. Do you feel a tree working in this role? What is the tree guarding?

Figure 13.1. Photograph of the guardian white oak at Allen's Creek, IN, and younger trees grown up around it.

The general character of trees may be invoked for symbolic power, such as part of a sacred center, to hold sacred space, and/or as a conduit for shamanic work. A large tree near or in a ceremony site could symbolize the World Tree for the purpose of the work. Black Bear Grove developed strong relationships with a huge old beech tree at a Hoosier National Forest ceremony site and a large northern red oak at a ridgetop site in the Allen's Creek Recreation Area.

Specific tree species may be invoked based on their properties. For example, holly may be invoked for its power as an evergreen and for its association with fire as Tinne in the Tree Ogham.

T13.8. Interact regularly with trees.
Ongoing relationships with trees are an important part of my practice. I converse with them, dance among them, give praise offerings, bow, give them Reiki, and enter into agreements with them. There are many ways that we can interact with trees.

When I lived in Bloomington, IN, I would do my Qi Gong set in the shade of a large black cherry. I would bow and give offerings to the tree regularly. Occasionally, I would ask the cherry for wisdom in my business dealings. A large ash in Bryan Park was another favorite to work with. I would regularly walk circles around this tree and do the Tsalagi Dance with it. Many fond memories and feelings of gratitude are welling up in me as I reflect and write about these relationships. I strongly recommend spending time with a tree.

Figure 13.2. Ash (*Fraxinus sp*) in Bryan Park, Bloomington, IN. This tree was a regular companion for me during my spiritual practice.

T13.9. Protect the trees.

Dedicated individuals sit in trees for months to prevent them from being cut down. Prometheus, an old northern red oak in Yellowwood State Forest, avoided being cut down because an organized tree sit prevented the logging of the area. Tree and forest stewardship has been a focus of many organizations such as Heartwood and Indiana Forest Alliance. We find additional heroes in literature to further inspire us toward stewardship, such as the Ents in the Lord of the Rings Trilogy (Tolkien, 1954), or the Lorax of Dr. Seuss (1971).

Trees are the breath of the planet and they can remind us of the general character of our environment or even spiritual health. Small white tree spirits came back to the forest during its regeneration after near total destruction in the animated film Princess Mononoke (Miyazaki, 1997). Let's honor those spirits and do right by the trees.

"Trees are poems that the earth writes upon the sky" Kahlil Gibran

CHAPTER 14. Stories, poetry, and song.

"A Naturalist is someone who, when treed by a bear, enjoys the view" Anonymous

T14.1. Bear stories.
Magic can happen in a gathering of friends around a campfire. As we enjoy each other's company and chat around the fire, sometimes the conversation topic can wander to bear encounters. For me, bear stories are treasures of the campfire. The stories are rarely as interesting as the emotions of the story tellers as they relive the experiences.

A very brief but memorable encounter with a black bear (*Ursus americanus*) occurred on Iron Mountain in Virginia. When I crested the shoulder of the mountain, I saw a bear moving so fast that he appeared to me as a black streak. He impressed me with the noise he made while crashing through young trees and with his speed. This bear was an omen linked to an important phase of development in Black Bear Grove of Ár nDraíocht Féin (ADF).

Another time, while backpacking along the Appalachian Trail in Georgia, a buddy and I encountered bears in a pine stand with no understory trees but with a very thick shrub layer. Momma bear reared up on her hind legs so that her head and torso were up above the shrub layer, I stated "bear" in a loud conversational tone, and then we heard rustling among the shrubs. A split second later a cub emerged out of the shrub layer and scampered up a tree between us and the momma bear. I felt fear rising within me as I thought of appearing as a threat to the cub. I did not particularly desire to feel bear claws ripping through my flesh (although that would certainly be a way of connecting with nature). Claws in the flesh did not come to pass. Instead, the momma bear made a loud grunt and the cub shot down the tree and away from us through the shrubs.

Sometimes we are blessed with multi-episode bear sagas. I encountered a big black bear along the road as I left a friend's house in New Hampshire. I had discovered a claw print from likely the same bear in my friend's driveway the day before.

I experienced a two day saga with a bear in the Adirondacks when I was a young Boy Scout. I witnessed another scout run up to the leaders' shelter and while out of breath explain that the corner of his tent was torn away by a bear – the bear had stolen marshmallows from the tent. The next morning I discovered the ravaged bear bag of our neighbors – only one third of the food remaining. They had hung their bear bag approximately 10 feet in the air but very close to the trunk of a tree. From the evidence at the scene, we speculated that the bear was able to sink a claw into the trunk of the tree and use this claw hold as leverage to get up high enough and swat the bag down. Later in the morning, as I watched the older scouts rehanging the bear bag, the bear came sauntering down into the camp. Kids banged pots and pans. The bear sniffed the air a bit and then sauntered off.

While flying over the barrens of northern Canada in a helicopter, I was gifted with the site of the food cache of a grizzly. Part of the bear's future meal plans, the leg of a caribou, jutted up from the overturned Earth. Later, we encountered a large blonde grizzly loping across the tundra. The food cache came up as an image in my third eye (chakra located at the forehead) 18 years later in a shamanic journey.

Other nature stories are good "round the fire" fare as well. Snake stories are fun to tell and hear, likely due to the danger involved. I heard one of my favorite jokes around the fire: "What did the snail say while riding on the turtle's back? Weeeeeeeeee!" (Hissom, 1999)

T14.2. Chant.
Chants can be used to raise energy in personal or group ritual, as offerings, as part of meditative and shamanic techniques, and in ad hoc combinations of methods.

> E pele e
> Ke akua [Wahine] o ka [na] puhaku ʻena ʻena
> ʻEli ʻeli kau mai
> (Oh Pele, goddess of the burning stones, let [a profound] [wonder and] awe possess me)
> > Traditional Hawaiian Oli (chant)
> > (Lockwood and Hazlett, 2010; Johnsen, 2013)

Elemental chants are used for celebrating nature as well as solar and lunar cycles.

> Earth my body
> Water my blood
> Air my breath
> Fire my spirit
> Earth my body
> Water my blood
> Air my breath
> Fire my spirit
> I am born of the elements
> I am born of the elements
> > Traditional with two lines added by Spiral Rhythm
> > > (Spiral Rhythm, 2001)

There are many existing nature-oriented chants that can be incorporated into your work, and it may be enlivening to write one that is customized to your ceremonial purposes. The following chant was written in late winter, expressing a desire to see and feel more direct sunlight and experience more daylight hours again.

> Sun, Sun, Sun, Sun
> Return to us
> Shine upon our dormant limbs
> Bring us new life

The chant empathizes with trees in late winter in addition to calling back the Sun.

T14.3. Devotional singing.
Allow devotional singing to escape your lips, inspired by land and spirit (like you might sing a hymn in church or kirtan).

> I am comin' home to the Appalachian Mountains
> I am comin' home
> I scrounge for food with the black bear
> I tumble down the bed of a mountain stream
> I soar like a turkey vulture
> And howl with coyotes
> Comin' home
> I am travelin' to the Appalachian Mountains
> Travelin' home
> I'm comin' home to the Appalachian Mountains
> Comin' home
>
> Climbing sandstone bluffs
> Dancing with the chestnut oak and hickory
> Blooming azaleas and mountain laurel
> Rooted in those thin mountain soils
> Looking out over the hollow
> Scarlet tanager sing with me
> Travelin' to the Appalachian Mountains
> I am travelin' home
> Comin' home to the Appalachian Mountains
> I am comin' home

This devotional song is improvisational and the verses come in the moment. There are an infinite number of verses with a finite amount of time to sing them.

Another improvisational devotional hymn is an ode to the trees that most recently went something like this:

> O' mighty oak. Strong and tall.
> Hickory, tough and resourceful.
> O' *Carya cordiformis* with bright yellow bud and bitter nut.
> Chestnut oak, thank you for livin' on the ridge.
> Big inspiring acorns.
> Sycamore, cottonwood, willow.
> Dwellin' in the wet soil.
> Hail your soggy roots.
> Sun loving sumac at the field edge.
> Friends in the old fields.
> Dogwoods bloomin' in the understory.
> Tall, straight tulip poplar.
> Oh, black locust, I taste your sweet blossoms.
> Many sacred trees, I see the divinity in you.

I like to use songs or chants when invoking specific aspects of nature in ceremonies. Devotional hymns make good praise offerings and can be part of our dialogue with nature. They can also help us open our joy channels and approach nature connection with an uplifted spirit.

T14.4. Tone baby tone.

In western Massachusetts, I met several folks who tone as a way of connecting with a natural area. They seem to use the toning as a type of sonar – letting it resonate within them and with the land. I eventually gave it a try and found it to expand my ability to explore – I sense how the sound comes back to me and how it resonates within me uniquely in that area. This practice follows the same principle as the ritual technique of toning or chanting "om" to get all the individual participants plugged into and resonating with the group.

T14.5. Read and write poetry.

Examples of nature inspired poetry are many. Some hiking clubs host poetry hikes to combine the poetry art form with moving through the landscape. Poetry allows exploration and expression of aspects of nature that other media leave out. See Chapter 15 for some nature poetry references.

Talking as part of a panel on Earth spirituality at Potomac Overlook Park in Virginia, I said I enjoyed being one with nature and right at that moment I felt bird poop land on my leg. The people were entertained.

CHAPTER 15. Inspirational readings.

We can connect with nature through the words of others and through affirmations.

T15.1. Read inspirational words.

I highly recommend the collection titled "Earth Prayers". It contains excellent content from many authors. This book provides me with a sense of the many different times, parts, occasions, and aspects of the Earth that we connect with as well as the many ways to do it. It covers a variety of occasions, purposes, and circumstances. It draws from many cultures.

"Thinking Like a Mountain" is a classic. It contains Chief Seattle's message, an academic style piece by Arnie Naess, and the passion of Joanna Macy and John Seed.

Poets Walt Whitman, Mary Oliver, Wendell Berry, and Rumi all have poetry with inspirational nature threads. Robert Frost wrote several poems that hit me in the gut and mind at the same time.

I also highly recommend the autobiography called "My Life with the Spirits" (Duquette, 1999). It does a great job of demonstrating a dialogue with the spirit world.

There are good, fast reading novels that highlight some of the concepts or techniques covered in this book. In the fantasy genre, Charles de Lint has brought a number of mystical nature entities to life in his magical books. For example, "Greenmantle" (de Lint, 1998) is an exploration of both Green Man and Horned God archetypes. Edward Abbey's classic "The Monkey Wrench Gang" speaks to the passion that can be involved in environmental activism. "Ecotopia" (Callenbach,1975) provides some food for thought regarding potential sustainable societies. Myths and legends make excellent reading as well.

Books focusing on individual species (e.g., loons, elephants, etc.) or aspects of wildlife [e.g., sexual reproduction in dioecious trees (species with male and female trees such as *Ginkgo biloba*)] can be very inspirational. If a particular animal resonates with you, you may want to learn more about the animal's habitat and behavior. Trailside notes or Naturalist musings can be similarly inspirational. John Muir is a great author in this regard. He has some classically eloquent and beautiful ways of discussing nature's beauty with the written word.

"Silent Spring" (Carson, 1962) is a classic work that helped to enhance awareness of our deteriorating environment in North America. The Sand County Almanac (Leopold, 1949) is another classic that expresses nature appreciation and respect. "Earth in the Balance" (Gore, 2000) is one of many publications that describe the totality of human influence on the environment. The high level of human influence on the Earth system has caused geologists to name our current geologic time period the "Anthropocene" (Zalasiewicz et al., 2008). Calls for greater respect for our environment are often based on the awareness of our tremendous impact combined with a sense of how precious nature and our environment are to us.

Books and other writings that contain tips for sustainable living can be inspiring because they give us practical options for "making a difference", from environmentally friendly cleaners (Logan, 1997) to tips for maintaining a seed bank. In a somewhat related vein, I have enjoyed reading The Backwoodsman Magazine because I find outdoor survival tips inspiring. I also enjoy news about sustainable technology because it gives me hope.

If you are motivated to work for environmental protection, including in the political realm, you may find environmental news stimulating. Greenwire, Defender's of Wildlife, Green Scissors, and the League of Conservation Voters are all organizations with websites that can plug you into environmental issues and the politics of them. Be warned that, while there are benefits of high environmental awareness, exposure to environmental news on a regular basis can lead to or contribute to depression, because the outlook for a healthy environment for many living creatures (including humans) is poor.

One or more of the many available nature writings may be able to provide inspiration or nourishment for your relationships with nature.

CHAPTER 16. Connecting through art.

Many examples of nature-inspired art exist. Artwork can express sentiments toward nature, celebrate beauty and diversity, and be a token of reverence or prayer. Nature art occurs in many forms:

- Photographs posted online and published in more traditional ways
- Drawings or paintings of scenes or aspects of nature
- Sculptures of nature beings or that work with the landscape they reside in
- Inspired garden design
- Landscape architecture in a broader sense (e.g., city parks designed by Frederick Law Olmsted such as Central Park in Manhattan)
- Architecture designed to highlight or work with nature (Frank Lloyd Wright homes)
- Dance
- Installations

Photographs by Ansel Adams and other nature photographers convey some of nature's intangible beauty. They inspire us, tantalize us, and motivate us to get out into the wild, and they can help "get us through" until we can get there. We use nature images for our computer screen backgrounds even as we also try to get an office with a window. We have paintings and prints of nature hanging on our walls. We celebrate and converse about nature by sharing images. Nature photographs are taken and posted in many venues, including on Facebook (a social networking website) and photograph sharing websites. Combining spiritual quotes with artwork and photographs is a way of galvanizing a positive nature message.

Art expresses our emotional and spiritual relationships with nature in beautiful, cathartic ways. And we can enhance our personal connection through participating in various forms of artwork.

T16.1. Create an installation as part of nature.
Simple rock cairns as well as more formal shrines and memorials are erected to honor specific aspects of nature, for celebrations, and for religious ceremonies. Folks build stacks of stones in various locations in the landscape (e.g., on gravel bars in creeks). Setting up temporary altars in ritual space is another artistic installation, and creatively decorating the altars can link a celebrant to a ceremony in a unique way. Sculptures, paintings, and sketches can all mark the sacredness of place and time. Making an Earth Mother (Nerthus) figure from clay on the shore of Lake Monroe, IN, for a solstice celebration in 2004 involved deep emotional and spiritual work with the lake, shoreline, and archetype of Earth Mother. The artist described the sculpting of Nerthus as his main personal ritual work of the ceremony. More permanent shrines of specific nature entities or the land in general are found at many nature sanctuaries (e.g., Lothlorien and Wisteria), and some long-term worship sites within landscapes have altars and sculptures (e.g., the Nemeton at Brushwood Folklore Center in western New York State). Labyrinth design is a form of landscape architecture that can work with the local land – see Figure 7.1.

Contributions to the energy that come from heartfelt creativity are beautiful to experience. Drawing and making masks for workshops gives the experience an added dimension and an enhanced personal participation for those involved. Creative costumes and altar decorations also enhance participation in ceremonies or workshops. Artistic effort put into offerings for aspects of nature can be very rewarding as well.

The artwork of Beth and Zeeb is a testimony to the primal and magical energies of nature. They use found aspects of nature (e.g., roots of small dead trees) in their art. They create beautiful fairy figurines that highlight the mystique and beauty of nature (Beth and Zeeb, 2013). Totem poles are another type of sculpture with magical significance. Among indigenous cultures, totem poles were a symbol of status and showed identifying characteristics of a chief or other persons of high station. In modern North American society, making a totem pole can be a way of learning about self and working with specific guiding influences. One man told me that sculpting a totem pole had been a healing influence as well as a rite of passage for him.

Expressing oneself and learning through art is a way of finding personal fulfillment while also enlivening those who experience the finished product.

CHAPTER 17. Cultural lenses.

"The breath of the dragon, that came before time, gave birth to all things."
Stormdragon

As a result of their heritage and upbringing, people relate to nature through specific cultural lenses (aspects of culture that influence the way we observe, sense, and interact). These lenses can help us look at phenomena with different perspectives and help us learn in multiple modes. Myths and stories, religious teachings, family teachings, institutional education, deities and archetypes with whom we work, symbols, and personal experience all provide background for working with nature. Cross-cultural influences and unique aspects of individual cultures shape the paths that people take through life. The perspectives and skills associated with each individual spiritual path contribute to the richness that we experience when we come together in groups to connect with the land. Hail cultural diversity!

Stories, legends, chants, songs, poems, and lore

As we now live in the "time of the great mingling" (Waterhawk, 2002), increased access to information makes a great diversity of folklore available to us. Cultural lore of rocks, minerals, animals, and plants as well as lore from regions and localities are all at our fingertips. The world's religions and other pillars of culture provide us with stories and icons that can inform our experience of nature. Creation stories are associated with specific places, landforms, nature beings, and/or all of existence. Other stories depict significant events and/or are legends associated with specific places. Legends can broaden our perspective about aspects of nature. They give us new lenses with which to view the land.

One of my favorite creation stories involves the formation of the Appalachian Mountains by a "Great Buzzard". The vulture flew across the Earth when it was new (still soft mud). As the vulture's wings flapped downward touching the Earth (due to fatigue related to having crossed the ocean, according to one telling), the valleys and mountains were created (Indians.org, 2013). Another telling explains how the vulture formed the Valley and Ridge Province of the Appalachians by flying close to the Earth such that when the bird's powerful wings beat down they carved a valley, and when they came back up a linear area was left undisturbed and became a ridge. The next downward wing movement created the next valley, and wings coming back up allowed high ground to remain. In this manner, the wing action of the vulture created the alternating long valleys and ridges of the Valley and Ridge Province as the bird flew inland.

Minerals and particular occurrences of minerals have creation stories as well. Twinned staurolite crystals (twinning involves two crystals growing from the same point) in "x" and "+" shapes are called "fairy crosses", especially those from a specific location within Patrick County, VA. Local legend has it that one day long ago fairies were playing around in a spring when an elfin messenger brought them the news of the crucifixion of Jesus Christ. The fairies wept in response to the news of Christ's death and the teardrops crystallized in the form of the cross as they fell to the Earth (Kunz, 1913).

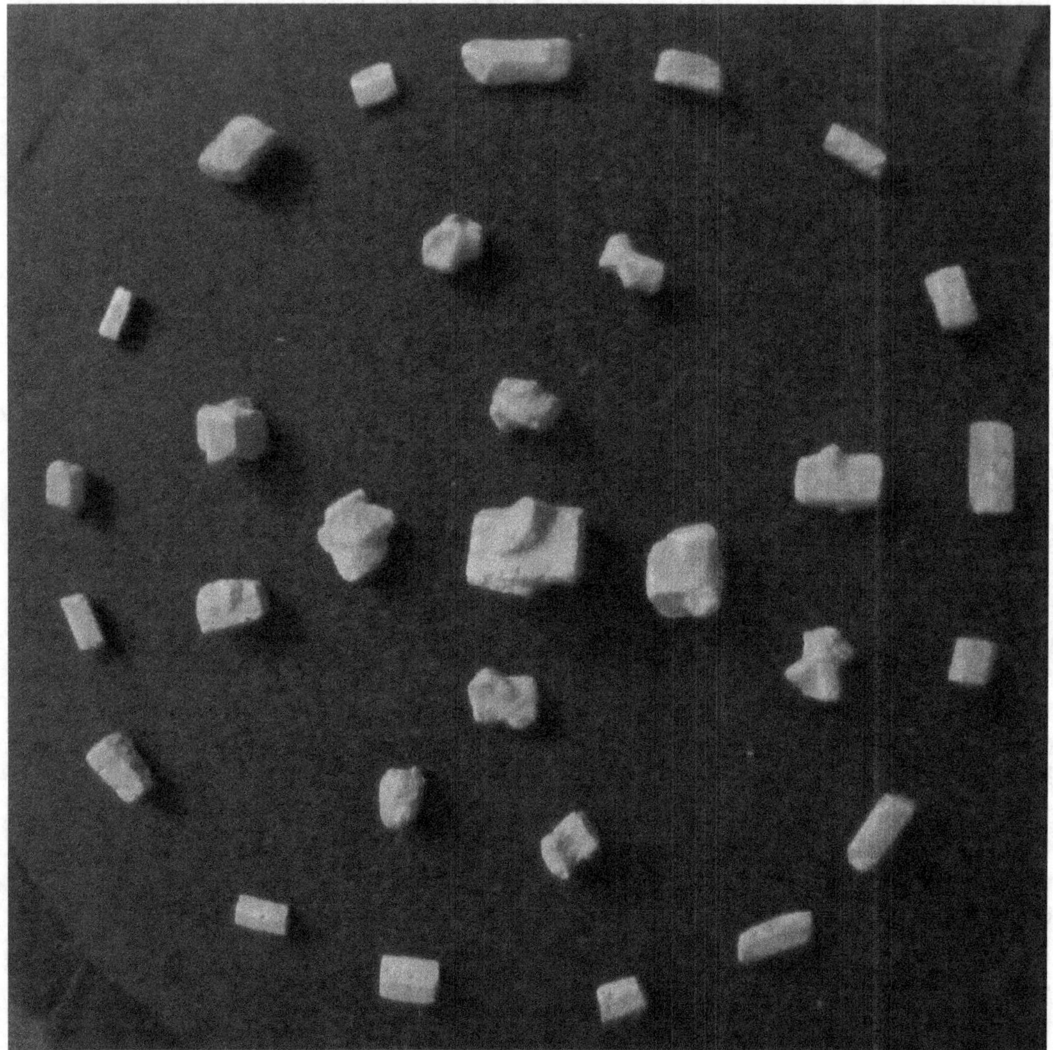

Figure 17.1. Twinned staurolite crystals collected in Patrick County, VA. A ring of single, non-twinned staurolite crystals encircles the fairy crosses.

Amethyst was created as the god Bacchus set his tigers upon a young girl. He had been offended by a lack of consideration in another matter, and in response to these feelings he became determined to kill the first person he met. This happened to be a young maiden named Amethyst who was on her way to worship at Diana's temple. When the tigers sprang upon Amethyst, she appealed to Diana for help, and Diana turned her into a clear crystal so that she would be safe. Bacchus poured the juice of grapes over Amethyst to soothe her in repentance for his crime. The juice gave the crystal a purple hue (Jangl and Jangl, 1985).

Plants also have creation stories. For example, anemones are the tears Venus shed for Adonis (Jones, 2013). In the Hawaiian creation story "Kumulipo", the taro plant was created first by Papa and Wākea (Earth and sky beings) and humans were created second (Fields, 2009). Plants are involved in European legends as well. In an effort to protect her son Balder, the Norse goddess Frigg made a deal with nature beings so that they would not hurt her son. She made this deal with all except Mistletoe, and of course a dart of mistletoe is what killed Balder (Crossley-Holland, 1980).

In one version of the Ganges River creation story, Ganga comes to Earth from the heavens to rescue tormented souls. Shiva was asked to intercept her because her raw power was predicted to have a devastating effect. Shiva caught Ganga in his hair as he stood on a mountain top, and after a while seven streams were allowed through, the seventh becoming the Ganges River (Colum, 1930).

Animal characters are prominent in Native American and African myths (Cooper, 1993; Willis, 1993a). In Native American traditions, animal spirits are key players in important cultural developments. As legend has it, the Native American flute, one of the world's oldest instruments, was given to the people by the Woodpecker (Lane, 2013). The gift of the pipe to the Lakota by the White Buffalo Woman is the story behind one of the key Lakota ceremonies – the Pipe Ceremony (Cooper, 1993). A number of animal spirits (Raven in the Pacific Northwest, Spider in the plains states, and Coyote in the Southwest) were considered tricksters, and had important roles to play in creation stories. In addition to playing tricks, Coyote used his cunning to bring fire to the people (with Turtle) in one myth and seeds to many tribes in another (Cooper, 1993; Wilkinson and Philip, 2007). The African spider deity Anansi is another well known animal trickster (Wilkinson and Philip, 2007).

Diverse cultures (indigenous and otherwise) contain a variety of chants, songs, prose, and poetry used for centuries or millennia in ceremonies and various other aspects of life. These can be complementary to stories and historical accounts for representing the weavings of culture through time.

Other rich devotional traditions include the Hindu tradition of kirtan, which is a call and response form of devotional singing, and folk songs and poems of the American environmental and back to the land movements. Traditional songs are often inserted into modern North American ceremonies. Examples of devotional songs and chants are included in Chapter 14 and sprinkled throughout the book.

Legends involving humans and the landscape can also be inspiring. Camping in West Virginia, I woke up to see a steep ridge of sandstone protruding up from the fog in the valley. This outcropping of the Tuscarora Sandstone resembled the spine of a dragon. At that time, at the Seneca Rocks trailhead, a plaque was present that described a Native American legend associated with that formidable spine of sandstone. As legend has it, Snow Bird, daughter of Chief Bald Eagle of the Seneca, challenged the men courting her to a climb up Seneca Rocks. She promised her hand, love, and life to the one that could make the climb. Seven men started out following her as she climbed. Three turned back as the difficulty increased. Two others could not make it beyond the fifth pinnacle of Seneca Rocks. One of the remaining two made it to within inches of where Snow Bird was on the summit, then began to fall, she caught him, they were wed, and Chief Bald Eagle made his son-in-law the successor as chief (Forest Service, 2013).

The story of the Great Flood and Noah's response is a popular piece of Christian theology. Blessed by the divine, Noah was able to help animal life continue on Earth despite the great catastrophe of the flood (Genesis 6-8). The story emphasizes the importance of diversity in nature.

"Cultural stories … describing relationships between humans and nonhumans, carry ancient knowledge still relevant to us today, and can also serve as a bridge between contemporary scientific inquiry and deeply embedded animistic spiritual sensibilities." *Tina Fields*

Archetypes, spirits, and deities

Just as myths and legends can help us connect, so also can working with archetypes, deities, and spirits. Aspects of the divine have been identified and worshipped in a variety of ways. If we look beyond attachments we have to a particular theology, we can find a tremendous richness in interacting with a variety of beings with a variety of names. We can also find an abundance of religious practices to choose from to connect with these spirits. Opportunities abound.

Deities are associated with natural forces, energy movements, and energy sources (e.g., river goddesses, gods and goddesses of volcanic activity, woodland horned gods, green men, wind gods, Sun gods and goddesses, Moon goddesses and gods, and thunderers). Deities are also associated with the Earth System as a whole as well as the Universe as a whole.

Great Spirit creator deities are common among Native American traditions. For example, Manitou of the Algonkin people and Wakan Tanka (Grandfather) of the Lakota. Corn gods and goddesses were common among North American tribes, sometimes being linked to the "all" deity (Cooper, 1993). Omniscient All Father and creator types exist in other cultures as well (e.g., the modern Christian God, Allah, and Odin of the Norse). Hindu mythology has a threesome as its creator, all, and lord of all deities: Brahma, Vishnu, and Siva respectively (Wilkinson and Philip, 2007). Christians celebrate the beauty of nature as a wondrous gift from the creator. My uncle led an exercise in which he had his Sunday school students break apart layers of shale and look at the newly exposed rock surfaces. He asked them to contemplate that nobody else had ever seen what they were seeing. The Earth is beautiful, complex, and diverse.

In addition to the All Father, there are deities who are linked to large portions of the Earth System. Earth Mother deities have been worshipped across the globe. Nerthus was worshiped by the tribes along the Elbe River. The Roman Historian Tacitus wrote one of the oldest surviving records of an Earth Mother ritual. According to his account, essentially seven Germanic tribes (Reudingi, Aviones, Anglii, Varini, Eudoses, Suarini, and Nuitones) had a common form of worship of Nerthus, or Mother Earth. Their worship involved working with a representation of Nerthus which only a priest could touch, was veiled under a cloth, and resided in a cart in a sacred grove on an island in the ocean for much of the year. When the priest perceived Nerthus' presence, her cart was subsequently pulled by cows among the people. The people celebrated each place she went and there was no war. "… then, and only then, are peace and quiet known and loved, until the priest again restores the goddess to her temple, when she has had her fill of human company. After that the cart, the cloth and, if you care to believe it, the goddess herself, are washed in a secluded lake" (Tacitus, circa 98). The full description of this ritual can be found in many different editions and translations of Tacitus' Germania and has been quoted many places online including Wikipedia (2013d). Pachamama is the Andean Earth Mother goddess established before the Inca Empire who farmers worshipped at altars in the middle of their fields (Wilkinson and Philip, 2007). Danu is the mother of the Irish gods. Grandmother is an Earth Mother of the Lakota (Cooper, 1993). I had the pleasure of interacting with a grandmother figure, whose belly was the Earth, in a guided visualization that took us away from the Earth and gave us a view from space. "Mother Earth" and "Mother Nature" are commonly referred to in modern English speech and similarly in other languages. Oberon Zell's Gaia embodies the archetype and tells the story of evolution of life on earth, as a progression of creatures is depicted moving from her feet upward toward her head. The Great Dragon is both creator and Earth. Mountains are the spine of the Dragon, and rivers are her veins.

Some Native Americans and some modern Neopagans work with a Sky Father and an Earth Mother, and several traditions celebrate the interaction between them. One common theme involves the Sky Father fertilizing the Earth Mother with rain and sunshine.

Weather related deities include wind gods (e.g., Stribog), and various thunder and lightning deities [Thunderbird (Lakota), Thor (Norse), Shango (Yoruba), Taranis (Celtic), and Baal (Canaanite)] (Wilkinson and Philip, 2007; Porter, 1993; Cooper, 1993). Hurricanes are named for a Taino and Carib god called "Huracan" or the Mayan storm god "Hunraken" (American Meteorological Society, 2012).

Many cultures have deities associated with the Sun. Belenos (Celtic), Ra (Egyptian), Apollo (Greek), and Utu (Sumerian) are all Sun gods; while Suna of the Norse and Sul of the Celts are Sun goddesses (Wilkinson and Philip, 2007). Sun gods and goddesses are worshipped in association with Earth's relationship with the Sun, resulting seasonal changes through the year, and changes through the day. Demeter and Persephone of the Greeks are associated with the winter and the growing season halves of the year. When Persephone goes into the underworld for half of the year, her mother Demeter morns and does not bring life to the plants. When Persephone returns, her mother celebrates, and plants blossom and bloom (Goldhill, 1993). So the emergence of Persephone is associated with spring. Eostre, from whom the Christian holiday of Easter gets its name, is a Germanic spring goddess known to appear as a hare (Mythology Dictionary, 2012). Myths also link to the Sun's daily path. Ra, Apollo, and Suna are all renowned for their travels across the sky.

Deities associated with the Moon include the Egyptian goddess Isis and a Saxon lunar god related to the Germanic tradition of the "Man in the Moon" (Jones and Pennick, 1995). Moon deities are invoked in rituals that engage with lunar energies and cycles.

Deities can be linked to landforms, The Dragon's spine is linked to mountain ranges. A butte in the Grand Canyon is named after the Hindu god Shiva, the schist exposed at the bottom of the canyon is called the Vishnu Schist after the Hindu deity Vishnu, and Manannan mac Lir is linked to the Isle of Mann. Nerthus comes to us from her island in the sea.

Goddesses have been associated with rivers in many cultures. For example, Buk is a stream and river goddess of the Sudanese (Mythology Dictionary, 2012), the Celtic Sequona is the goddess of the Seine River in France, and Matrona is the goddess of the Marne River (Roberts et al., 1997).

Gods and goddesses of the oceans have been important players in tribal cultures. Sedna is an Inuit goddess of the sea creatures that provide food for humans (Wilkinson and Philip, 2007). She appeared sitting on a cloud in a journey that I took during a crystal bowl event, but I didn't know who she was until another participant gave me her name based on my description. The message of the journey was clear: pay attention to the health of the oceans. Manannan mac Lir, a Celtic god of the shallow seas, has been a popular choice for the role of gatekeeper in Ár nDraíocht Féin rituals.

Deities are linked to plants. Diarmid is an Irish goddess who is the keeper of the herb lore, and Flora is a Roman flower and fertility goddess (Wilkinson and Philip, 2007). Nemetona is a Celtic goddess associated with sacred groves (nemetons) – important sites for Druidic traditions (Stewart, 1990).

Deities and Christian saints are linked to animals. Saint Francis is associated with birds and other animals. The Welsh goddess Rhiannon is linked to birds and horses. The Irish goddess "the Morrigan" is also known as "Battle Crow", and she appears as an eel in a myth involving the hero Cuchulain (Rolleston, 1917). The Welsh god Llew shape shifts into an eagle and his wife Blodeuwedd is turned into an owl (Jones and Jones, 1993). Odin has two ravens – Thought and Memory. Animals behave as divine beings in many Native American stories. In some stories, these divine animal spirits are considered separate from an extra divine group.

The "Lord of the Animals" archetype is present in many cultures and sometimes the same deity is associated with this archetype and with the hunt. Deities of the hunt include Herne the Hunter of the British Isles (an antlered deity), and the Roman Diana who is also associated with deer (Wilkinson and Philip, 2007).

Local deities and spirits have had a place in religious practices of many tribal cultures of antiquity. They also have a prominent place in some types of Druidry, modern Native American traditions, and other modern traditions. Entities called "nature spirits" are an important kindred of spirits in the practice of Ár nDraíocht Féin (ADF) Druidry. The Fairy or Fae tradition (modern and old traditions of the British

Isles and North America) works with spirits called fairies that dwell within the landscape. Norse traditions identify a category of spirits called "land wights". Native American traditions work with many beings of nature as spirits. Spirits of individual animals are a main thrust of many Native American stories and religious practices. The stone people and star people are invoked and honored in some Native American ceremonies. The regular dialogue with nature spirits of Native American traditions is a source of inspiration in my practice. See Chapter 21 for ideas for working with local spirits in rituals and ceremonies.

Green men are symbolic of nature's presence and are reputed to help people connect with nature. Foliate heads (green men) are a common celebration of nature in architecture and art (Matthews, 2002). The Green Man (aka Greenman) is also alive and well in cultural traditions and ceremonies practiced today. One festival in England has centered around a ritual in which green men symbolically slay the Jack-in-the-green to release the spring (Jack-in-the-green Festival Committee, 2013). Even though green men were largely a European tradition in the past, we can connect with local green men here in North America. Figure 17.1 depicts a sculpture that symbolizes a local North American Green Man. We can chant:

> Greenman, walking on the ridge, we hear your footsteps.
> Greenman, swimming in the lake, we flow with you.
> Greenman, dancing with the trees, we feel your strength within our hearts.
> Greenman, come and sit with us, help us honor you.
> Adam Davis, 2003

Figure 17.2. Green Man sculpted to include the leaves of North American trees accompanied by two smaller green men.

Horned deities can also help us connect with nature in a variety of ways. With Pan, we can get in touch with passions of nature. Pan also has a worldly aspect. Cernunnos, shown as lord of the animals in a famous image on the Gundestrup Cauldron (MacCana, 1985; MacInnes, 1993; Wikipedia, 2013c), is also a divine shaman. He has been a guide for journeys through the land, and is a member of the broader archetype of the Woodland God. During journeys to connect with my guiding spirits, I have worked with both small horned beings (probably local horned spirits) as well as green men of various shapes and sizes.

Making your own deity images helps forge a personalized connection with them. It can be part of the dialogue discussed in Chapter 6. The giving of offerings and making of prayers can be focused through a sculpture, painting, or other artwork that signifies the spirit or deity. In the Hindu tradition, this practice is called "puja". Creating this focus is a way of being present with and doing work with the deity or spirit.

Symbols

Talismans, symbols, and objects of power of many cultures can be linked to nature's materials and/or processes.

The symbol of the World Tree connects parts of religious cosmologies. Yggdrasil connects the worlds of the Norse (Crossley-Holland, 1980; Davidson, 1993). The Kabbalah links angels and properties of existence in a multidimensional tree of meaning. A modern World Tree can link all living things through a phylogenetic tree. Tree symbology shows up in many forms in the fabric of many cultures.

Rocks and minerals are also important societal symbols. Gemstones were chosen based on their metaphysical properties to decorate the Tabernacle as described in the Bible (Kozminsky, 1988; Kunz, 1913), and gemstones and minerals that are associated with zodiac signs in astrological traditions (birth stones) are sometimes incorporated into rings. Minerals have been used in healing practices by many cultures. For example, turquoise is known for its balancing and healing energy in some Native American traditions (Jangl and Jangl, 1985). See Chapter 12 for gemstone, rock, and mineral correspondences.

As discussed in Chapter 12 and indicated in cultural associations mentioned in this chapter, animals are used as symbols in a number of ways. The practice of working with spirit animals is common in Native American traditions and was important in European tribal traditions as well. Carr-Gomm et al. (1995) illustrates metaphysical and theological meanings of animals in Celtic traditions. Animals are associated with Chinese, Zoroastrian, and other zodiacs.

Traditions and practices

The Dragon Tradition is a mosaic of related traditions involving a single full Earth System dragon (known as "the Dragon") as well as multiple dragons (elemental as well as of specific areas). Practitioners of this tradition may work with and live the Dragon and/or work with dragons as metaphors for aspects of the Earth, among other options. A mountain ridge is the spine of the Dragon. The blood of the Dragon is the water that flows in the ground and in the rivers of the Earth. It is also the blood in our veins. The body of the Dragon has been linked to lines and places of power in the landscape.

There are many cultural traditions that involve devotional activities such as prayers, hymns, chanting, and vigils. Brigid's flame has been kept lit by nuns at Kildare in Ireland, and networks of folks across the globe have kept the flame lit through Brigid's candles. Prayers are made and songs are sung around fires, in sweat lodges, in churches and temples, and in the middle of the forest.

Physical offerings are another common devotional activity. The spirit houses in Thailand are small structures outside the home where offerings can be left for the local spirits. Tying offerings to trees is a multi-cultural tradition, done at Native American sites, at locations in pre-Christian and Christian Ireland, and other places. Offerings are left in the center of labyrinths. Offerings for Pele are left at the Volcano where she is thought to dwell in Hawaii (Fields, 2009).

Fairy and animal statues, and other objects, are installed as ornaments within lawns and in other places within landscapes. Some of these installations relate to folk traditions regarding local spirits. For example, gazing balls seen in rural lawns across North America are installed to protect against malevolent spirits.

Many societal and individual practices track Moon and Sun cycles. People feel the seasons that are determined by Earth's relationship with the Sun. Solar cycle based holidays are celebrated today and were celebrated by our ancestors. In modern times, eight major holidays honor the Sun as well as Sun and Earth relationships in the Northern hemisphere. Imbolc (Catholic Candlemas), Beltane (Mayday), Lughnasadh (Catholic Lammas), and Samhain (Halloween) are all holidays based on Celtic fire festivals of old. Solstices and equinoxes were and are celebrated by many cultures as well. These and other "turning of the wheel of the year" celebrations include fertility rites at the Celtic fire festival of Beltane (e.g., the passage of cattle and young maidens between two large fires), harvest celebrations in August through October, all night vigils at the winter solstice to ensure the return of the Sun, and various traditions associated with the Celtic fire festival of Imbolc (or Oimelc) that celebrate the beginning of spring when the ewes begin to make milk for the lambs (Jones and Pennick, 1995).

Lunar cycles are honored in a variety of ways, including for their influences on our bodies and energy cycles. Ritual purposes are often synced up with phases of the Moon: growth can be encouraged during waxing Moons, while death and letting go are more appropriate workings for the waning Moon.

Native Americans gather regularly to participate in and witness the Sundance. The Lakota are one tribe for whom the Sundance is a long standing tradition. In this dance, the dancers are connected to a sacred tree with rawhide chords, and they dance around the tree to the beat of drums (Neihardt, 1932).

Japanese gardens are part of a rich tradition of connecting with the land. In a number of these gardens, and in backyards of the people in Japan, Jizo appears. Jizo is a bodhisattva associated with equanimity, benevolence, courage, being fully responsible, being engaged with life, and being unquenchably optimistic (Peters, 2013). Jizo seems to appear and be placed in harmony with the contour of the land. "The representation of Jizo in this way in the natural environment could be interpreted as a vehicle for bringing the rich, nurturing energies of the Earth into the human (cultural) realm. Jizo is referred to as the Earth-store Bodhisattva which is a reference to the deep and rich, life-sustaining bounty of the natural environment" (Peters, 2013). Also, Jizo statues are placed to mark unexpected deaths of children and adults.

Figure 17.3. Jizo in a Japanese garden, Northampton, MA.

Places with cultural significance

Places have special significance to the world's religions: sometimes for natural character and sometimes for events that occurred there. In some cases, multiple religions have correspondences for the same place (e.g., Islam and Christianity in Jerusalem, and Pagans and Christians at Kildare, Ireland).

Temples and worship sites, both modern and ancient, of a variety of traditions (Buddhist, Hindu, Mayan, Incan, Egyptian, Greek, Roman, Celtic, Christian, Jewish, Muslim, Shinto, and other traditions) can be visited across the globe. In many cases, the choice of the site relates to the energies or energy of the land. Many past Native American ritual locations, marked or not, dot the landscape of North America. Mounds built by indigenous North American cultures from multiple time periods are prominent sacred sites in the Mississippi River Watershed. Some of these mounds are effigy mounds, built in the shape of and carrying the symbology of nature beings. Chapter 9 discusses some sacred sites of North America. Lines and networks of lines (e.g., ley lines) that connect sacred sites are also discussed in Chapter 9.

Religious faith, stories, and histories of sacred places help some people employ other techniques of this book. These cultural treasures can give us a glimpse of how some of our ancestors connected with the land and inspire creative ways to reinvent or reinvigorate traditions in ways that can serve us in modern times.

"As Pan Gu slept, his body became the mountains and his blood, the rivers"
Chinese Myth: Pan Gu and Nu Wa's Creation
(Wilkinson and Philip, 2007)

CHAPTER 18. Living close to the land.

When it comes to connecting with the land, there is no substitute for spending time in the wild.

T18.1. Take a hike.
Hiking in natural areas is a great way to explore the variety of beings and processes occurring in the landscape. A regular hiking practice works well with other techniques in the book, such as tracking a place through the seasons and finding power spots within the landscape. You can hike out to places and do a deepening technique (e.g., meditating on El Capitan in Yosemite National Park). Many of the immersion techniques in Chapter 10 (such as bushwhacking) can be done while out hiking.

T18.2. Practice orienteering.
Using various ways of navigating (especially with Sun, Moon, and stars) is another unique way to connect with the land. This activity can help you realize your place in the landscape and help you understand the interrelatedness of the many forces and beings that occur in the area. Navigating various ways through a landscape can help you see the whole.

T18.3. Go camping.
Sleeping in a tent connects you with the lay of the land, because you get familiar with natural wind breaks and drainage patterns. Pitching your tent on high ground that does not feel the full force of storms is recommended. You might not enjoy some of the results of pitching your tent in the divots or stream channels of the landscape.

Camping can bring us closer to insects, can result in bear encounters, and can get us more involved with protecting our food and getting clean water to drink. We are also more closely in touch with our impacts on the system. Please limit impacts by reusing camping sites and fire pits and preventing unnecessary disturbances of the ecosystem. See Leave No Trace (2013) for tips on practicing low impact camping.

T18.4. Go backpacking.
Backpacking trips combine the benefits of physically journeying through the landscape with all of the personal day to day survival tasks that are highlighted through camping.

T18.5. Build your own shelter.
Building a shelter with materials found in nature gets us connected with the resources that are available in a particular area. It engages our knowledge of properties of trees and other plants. Sleeping under a modest shelter of fallen limbs in the wild connects us in a very different way than sleeping in a tent.

T18.6. Sleep out.
Sleeping out with no shelter is also a very rewarding way to connect. Animals can crawl across you during the night. Depending on where you are, mosquitos and/or other critters may be of concern. Falling asleep while gazing at the stars is an

experience whose value defies description.

T18.7. Poop in the woods.
When I am backpacking or hiking in the wilderness and I get the urge to lose some brown weight, I look around for two fallen trees crossing each other such that I can sling my legs over one and lean my back against the other and poop down into the gap between the logs. I enjoy the process of searching for and finding an ideal spot, and the added comfort that it provides. I enjoy gathering my wiping materials, prioritizing last year's fallen leaves and green leaves of invasive plants next. I don't recommend using poison ivy for wiping your butt. Even if I have to lean against a tree or squat with no support, I enjoy that I am doing an important part of life without the crutches of modern society.

We can start to get to know the land through hiking, camping, backpacking, sleeping out, and pooping in the woods; and we can connect more deeply by working with the land for our survival. We can cultivate survival skills by integrating them into our daily lives, and we can practice them in the wilderness.

We can learn about and work with the aspects of nature that provide us with water and food in wild areas or through cultivation. Techniques include:

- **T18.8. Find water.** The ability to find water involves knowing where water occurs in the landscape. Locations of water sources relate to the lay of the land, drainage patterns, and amount of rainfall.
- **T18.9. Forage for food.** Grazing, picking a salad, and making meals from roots and greens all plug me in to a place in a special way. I ingest the essence of soil and groundwater when I graze the chickweed or violets from a gap community in a temperate forest. As part of the foraging process, I make sure to ask the place if it is OK to eat plants from that location and I keep an eye on the sustainability of that species in the area. I use a combination of the word of a fellow Naturalist, an edible plants guide like Peterson (1977), and my tree and wildflower plant identification system to assess whether plants are edible, and then I partake. I love foraging by myself, but I also enjoy doing it with others and have fond memories of foraging for chanterelle mushrooms with a dear friend in southern Indiana. I like to bring wild edibles to potluck gatherings. Picking wild greens works well as a salad dish for these types of gatherings. Stir fried buds, seed pods, and stems are also good food-sharing choices. Stir fried day lily buds were a big hit at a potluck one year at the Sirius Rising Festival in western New York State. I like to know which wild edibles are available in various regions of North America and during what times of year. I enjoy being in the North Woods in the summertime during blueberry season.

Figure 18.1. Bunchberries (a) and blueberries (b) of central New Hampshire.

- **T18.10. Hunt and trap.** Trapping or hunting your own food helps you learn patterns of animal behavior (e.g., where species are in the landscape at different times of day and during different seasons). Greater connectivity with the land can be achieved by using hunting tools and snares made from natural materials. Like with our many other activities that involve the sacrifice of others, we can acknowledge and have respectful dialogue with those that have sacrificed as well as the broader ecosystem. We can honor those that die so that we can live. In many cases, life requires death.
- **T18.11. Garden.** Working with soil can have a grounding and centering effect on our psyches. I feel much more connected with life when I am growing plants for food, especially when I am using compost to fertilize and when I make time to ask the land: "what should be planted where?" Landscaped areas and edge areas can be managed using permaculture principles in a way that provides food. This can be done sustainably and in a way that works with the land. We can grow food instead of lawns.
- **T18.12. Farm.** Farming can be done sustainably with crop rotation, composting, and no till techniques that do not involve chemical fertilizers or pesticides. Farming and eating organically encourage sustainability and health. Cerier (2013) highlights artistic possibilities related to preparing organic foods.

These techniques help us know our food and reduce the size of our foodshed (the foodshed concept is discussed in Chapter 2). We can garden, farm, hunt, and forage in ways that show as much respect and reverence as possible.

After food is in our bellies and we are in a relatively healthy state, we look to get warm, to be sheltered from the elements, to make better survival tools, and to learn better techniques for survival.

T18.13. To build a fire.
One of my favorite short stories is "To build a fire" by Jack London (London, 1908). It

reminds me of the importance of warmth for survival in certain situations (a winter day in the Yukon Territory in the story) and in turn reveals the true gift and privilege of fire. The story also reminds me that building a fire requires working with the land, including the current conditions and the materials available.

When we are out in the wild, a fire of some sort may be important for cooking our food. Building a fire from local materials gets us in touch with the area in a different way than if we use a camp stove. We can learn where tinder and kindling materials are and can ponder related workings of the ecosystem. We can go as far as creating fire from bow drill or flint and steel. If I need to work with large logs, I relish the opportunity to split wood, because it is both a meditative and enlivening activity for me. Using a fire that you built to cook food that you caught or foraged and then keeping warm with that fire into the night is a reminder of the primal components of survival and an affirmation that you have the skills to survive in the wild.

Just as in the London story, a successful fire involves working with the conditions and materials of the local area. Conversations with land, wood, and fire in its fledgling stages are beneficial. My scoutmaster introduced me to the importance of dialogue with the land through the way that he showed me how to build a fire. Even though I do it differently and have my own style, his teaching is still the essence of my fire building technique. He showed me how to work with the land, work with the conditions, be reverent of the element of fire, and know how it behaves. He taught me to respect the sacred fire.

Dialogue with the fire is part of a broader dialogue with nature. When collecting tinder, kindling, and larger wood from the ecosystem, I like to talk with nature entities and energies, seek synergy or at least permission, and receive guidance regarding how to find the right ingredients for the fire. I have been shown the missing ingredient in pre-fire structures of others by simply asking local beings what is missing, after showing them respect and giving them offerings, of course. Fire is a gift, a concept which can be kept in mind when asking for fire before ceremonies or cooking. Be prepared to go without fire when you receive a "no" answer.

T18.14. Make tools with nature's materials.
We can also work with nature's materials to make tools for survival. Knives, arrowheads, and axes can be made by knapping chert, flint, or certain volcanic rocks. Specific shrubs are good for arrow shafts (e.g., *Viburnum sp*), and some trees are good for bows [e.g., Osage orange – aka hedge apple (Whitefeather, 2004)]. Other plants are good for making twine or rope (e.g., dead milkweed stems).

We can integrate the practice of these skills into our daily lives to some degree. We can build fires in our backyards or fireplaces, and we can graze edible plants from our lawns (ideally lawns that have been pesticide free for at least five years).

T18.15. Ramp up and practice survival skills.
You can build the skills mentioned in this chapter by trial and error, and from written references, but it is usually easier to learn from others. Doing it through classes and with groups is ideal. If the idea of a survival course resonates with you, I suggest

working with a mentor who can help you ascertain the course and teacher that is right for you, since numerous schools and individuals teach survival skills. All the folks who I know who took courses taught by Tom Brown Jr. seemed to internalize the skills they learned and were inspired to continue to practice them. A number of Tom Brown Jr. students created courses and/or schools of their own. The Vermont Wilderness School is one example of a Tom Brown Jr. influenced organization.

Survival guides can be helpful for reminders and building upon skills you have learned from others. Self teaching does work but takes longer. It is easier if you find teachers or groups that are doing the work and can mentor you.

Living out in the wild for a long period of time (whether you are mainlining survival skills or not) can provide a number of feelings of being connected on a very deep level. The connectedness can manifest in interesting ways when you get back to society. Walking the Appalachian Trail is a 6 month immersion experience. "Through hikers" are in a different (more plugged in) state compared to others who are on the trail for shorter trips. They have cultivated a different energy through deep connection with the land. For me personally, I realized how my perspective had been altered after being in the barrens of northern Canada for close to 2 months. Coming back to Yellowknife and seeing an automobile, after not seeing one for weeks, was an alienating experience. Field work in a variety of professions, and the life of a wilderness hermit, can promote a deeply connected state.

While preparing for and engaging in survival efforts, and all of our other activities, we can use some of the sacred conversation and scanning for synergy techniques that are described in this book to be as respectful as possible. Awareness and communication can help us minimize our impacts and live in harmony with nature. We can seek mutual benefit, we can ask nature how best to do specific activities, we can give thanks, and we can ask what we can do to be of service.

CHAPTER 19. Environmental service.

Everyday actions are ways of connecting with the land. Being wasteful is a prayer of disregard for nature. Those of us who use more resources than the average global citizen, like many Americans do, are praying to encourage environmental and natural resource degradation. We continue to change the workings of the surface and atmospheric processes on our planet, including how fast aspects of the climate are changing and how water moves in our local watersheds.

Heal, Earth rapist!
And the clouds issue forth
Water rains down from the skies
Droplets touch down in the forest, grassland, and metropolitan madness

They collect on the surface of the brown beech leaf
On the surface of the bronze prairie grass
The water percolates down through the soil
Plants take it inside their roots
Animals drink from the water filled creek beds
The creatures are fed
The water flows through pores in the soil and out into a small stream channel
It moves along the bed
Getting stronger
Able to move bigger and bigger sand grains and pebbles
The land is cleansed

The stream flows into a bigger stream and then into the river
Water flows from cloud to soil to stream to river to the sea
And the land and its creatures are healed

The rain collects quickly
And flows as sheets along paved roads, sidewalks, and parking lots
Issuing forth from pipes
It rips into the bank
Tearing away the roots of the struggling young elm
The river swells quickly
Ripping away soil from its banks
Eroding the land of its birth
Water and mud spill into the landscape
Around the cypress grove and the sycamores
Flooding the farmers' fields and city streets
People are trapped in their cars
They are out of balance with nature
Unaware of the consequences of their lifestyles
Unaware that they can respect the spirits of the earth
Unaware that they too can heal
Adam Davis, 1/23/2004

The modern geological time period has been named the "Anthropocene" by some scientists based on the domination of human influence (Stromberg, 2013). People from many walks of life are expressing concern and alarm. They fear that human activities have impacted the Earth System so drastically that severe and unsolvable issues face human societies in the near future.

One aspect of human influence and domination is the extinction of other species. A number of scientists have suggested that we are in the midst of the largest extinction event in Earth history. We may want to reverse the trend if we want to connect with any of the threatened species in the future.

Another trend of concern is that current changes to Earth's climates are happening faster than the climate changes that occurred during the previous several hundred thousand years of Earth history. These rapid modern climate changes have been observed and felt in many areas of the globe, very strongly in high latitude ecosystems. Impacts and consequences of these changes are predicted to be large and widespread (IPCC, 2013). Predicted increases in the impacts from natural hazards as well as drought predicted for various areas are of particular concern. We are responsible for these changes, responsible for how we respond, and responsible for whether we are part of the solution or part of the problem going forward.

Doing environmental service is a way of connecting with nature, and it is a way of balancing or mitigating our personal impacts/footprint. Advocacy and conservation both engage our passions and our desire to do what is right. We have a chance to express our deep love for nature. Here are some options for service and how they can enhance our land relationship:

- **T19.1. Conduct clean-ups.** Picking up litter is an excellent, service oriented way of connecting with a particular place. I tend to prioritize recyclables and make sure they get recycled. This activity is fun to do with local environmental groups. All ages come together in community to take action for a better future.
- **T19.2. Prevent the spread of invasive species.** Departments of natural resources in a number of state governments have suggestions for minimizing the spread of invasive species: clean boots at trailheads before hiking; do not dump yard or household materials in the wild (dumping the contents of an aquarium in Lake Griffy, IN, was a possible culprit for the introduction of Brazilian elodea, which precipitated years of costly efforts to eradicate this foreign invasive plant); do not sell, transport, or burn ash as firewood to prevent the spread of the emerald ash borer; wash your boat before switching water bodies to prevent the spread of pests like zebra mussels; and other tips.
- **T19.3. Participate in invasive species pulls.** Removing invasive species helps preserve biological diversity which is linked to ecosystem health. When I participate in pulls, I experience philosophical dissonance. While I believe in the long term benefit for plant communities and ecosystems, I also question whether I have a right to judge which species lives or dies given the short 400

year tenure of my ancestors in North America. I advocate doing stewardship (including work with invasive species) via sacred conversations with an ecosystem or ecosystems.

- **T19.4. Practice and support land conservation.** There are many opportunities to help conserve and preserve lands. We can support parks, public land acquisition and conservation, and land trusts (e.g., the Sycamore Land Trust in southern Indiana). We can volunteer for or donate to a variety of organizations that do this type of work. One of the largest is The Nature Conservancy.
- **T19.5. Volunteer with watershed advocacy groups.** Examples include the Blackstone River Coalition and the Chesapeake Bay Foundation.
- **T19.6. Monitor logging, mining, and drilling companies.** Citizen groups monitor logging sales and cutting to make sure that best management practices are being followed. Volunteers can ensure that silt fences and ponds are in place, or that logging is not done on steep slopes.
- **T19.7. Be an active voice in natural resource management and environmental policy.** By cultivating an understanding of how things work in the Earth System, it becomes possible to be a wise voice in discussions about policies such as the sewer vs. septic debate in the Lake Monroe watershed, debates regarding whether to allow development in watersheds of drinking water reservoirs, decisions about whether to allow logging in state forests, and more.
- **T19.8. Support efficient salvage and waste management practices, and report illegal dumping.**
- **T19.9. Reduce, reuse, recycle.** This mantra promotes good consumer behavior and waste management, which reduce our footprints.
- **T19.10. Make smart personal choices to support sustainability.** We can make lifestyle choices that minimize our environmental impacts, and doing so is a way of being respectful of other inhabitants of the planet and praying for positive change. Here are some options:
  - Use lower footprint products and methods.
  - Reuse greywater in your house and yard.
  - Water lawn and garden from rain barrels, and/or from hoses attached to gutter systems.
  - Stop mowing.
  - Compost.
  - Make sustainable food choices such as eating locally grown foods, eating organically grown foods, and limiting meat meals.
  - Implement permaculture principles on your property.
  - Use less energy and fossil fuel:
    - drive less, walk, take the bus, and car pool.
    - turn down the thermostat in winter and up in summer.
    - turn off and unplug appliances when not in use.

  Sustainable lifestyle choices are available.
- **T19.11. Avoid using pesticides and chemical fertilizers.** These substances move from your lawn or fields down through the soil with the flow of groundwater and into streams and rivers. They are major threats to the

quality of water resources and health of aquatic ecosystems.
- **T19.12. Support societal efforts that encourage sustainability.** Quality initiatives include renewable energy, organic farming, land friendly local farming, waste to energy, composting, farmers' markets, local growers' guilds, smart land use decisions, and wild city initiatives.
- **T19.13. Be an environmental advocate.** Write politicians. Spread the word about issues. Ask for change.
- **T19.14. Engage in environmental activism.** Join environmental campaigns and organizations.
- **T19.15. Commit to land stewardship.**

Refer to Davis (2013c) for links for getting plugged into environmental service efforts, and a glimpse of the nature of organizations that are out there and that could benefit from your support.

Environmental service can be given as offerings to local and global nature spirits. Non-driving days are good offerings/sacrifices because they demonstrate respect and a desire to move toward a more sustainable lifestyle. For similar reasons, taking the bus and car pooling are also good offerings. Picking up and recycling litter in natural areas is another offering that can be made as part of an intentional relationship with these areas as well as the beings and processes in them. Oaths to improve the sustainability of our lifestyles, participate in specific conservation projects, and engage in advocacy also make good offerings. Stopping or speaking out against disrespectful or wasteful behavior is part of my oath of service to nature.

Physical offerings can be made in a smart way, keeping with our enhanced knowledge of the land. We can leave biodegradable offerings – such as a spirit plate of only organic foods. Water can be offered during a drought. Duct taping flowers to a tree is not an ideal offering – leaving the flowers at the base and conserving the duct tape would be better. In wild areas with a strong natural order, it may be better to give songs, prayers, and dances rather than physical offerings.

Getting and maintaining a level of environmental literacy is important for doing the best service possible. Working to better understand the connections between human activities and environmental issues within various ecosystems allows us to spend our service time wisely. Working with competent environmental groups as well as reading quality environmental literature can be helpful in this regard. Gore (2000) and introductory environmental science textbooks such as Cunningham and Cunningham (2010) are good starting points for cultivating an overall awareness of the status of our environment.

Our ongoing dialogue with nature can help us live with greater respect. Through dialogue, especially with physical processes of the land, we can understand cause and effect and therefore impacts of different kinds of land use. Through repeated connection with a variety of methods (including environmental science and policy scholarship) we can get better at advocacy, stewardship, right action, walking in balance, sustainable practices, and respect for the land and web of life.

CHAPTER 20. Humans working together.

Exploring nature connections with other people is extremely enlivening. We learn new techniques and ways of sensing nature through working with others because everyone has unique skills, energies, and experience to contribute. We can creatively combine our unique aptitudes for cultivating nature connections (which are related to mood, state of consciousness, background, integrity, and personal style) and grow spiritually in the process. We can complement each other in different ways and explore many potential synergies.

Chance meetings in nature can result in rich conversations. Among others, I enjoy talking with avid birders. They tell me which birds they have seen in the area and how bird presence varies seasonally. I have learned to identify birds, aspects of bird behavior, and about excellent science opportunities through talking with a variety of birders and Naturalists across North America. I was introduced to the common nighthawk by a Naturalist in Bloomington, IN. A birder filled me in on ducks commonly found at Fitzgerald Lake in Massachusetts. I will never forget my scoutmaster pointing out the loon wail the first time I heard it in the Adirondacks.

Chance meetings with folks in nature are very rewarding, and we can also connect more deliberately through planned events, classes, and groups. Examples include:

- Nature workshops at festivals or community fairs.
- Wildlife lectures and workshop series in parks.
- Wildflower and edible plant hikes. Naturalists lead wildflower hikes in a variety of natural areas across North America and across the globe. In the north central and northeastern USA, spring wildflower hikes are popular. In some areas, people enjoy seeing serviceberry, spring beauty, trout lily, larkspur, bloodroot, twinleaf, skunk cabbage, trillium, and other flowers blooming after the largely flower-free winter. In addition, the blooming of multiple species in desert ecosystems after a rain can be very enlivening.
- Hiking clubs. Members of hiking groups are into a mix of doing the work of the hike, connecting with others that are hiking, and experiencing aspects of the land they hike through. Some hikers use a mix of many approaches, while others mainline one or two. Some hikers focus on achieving the summit of a mountain, others on the psycho-spiritual journey of climb and descent, and others on enjoying the beings they interact with along the way.
- Survival classes and groups (see discussion in Chapter 18).

I have learned about birds, other animals, and plants through scheduled nature hikes and workshops of various types over the years. Comparing notes and getting feedback from others reinforces and broadens the knowledge base, making us better teachers, students, mentors, and mentees. Relationships that help us build knowledge affect our entire network of relationships.

Co-exploration of the land with others (including Naturalists, geologists, Druids, and folks from many other walks of life) has been tremendously valuable for my development. Some of the group connecting exercises discussed in Chapter 22 were inspired by ad hoc explorations at Ár nDraíocht Féin Naturalist retreats. Many of the techniques in this book come to me through ongoing work with others in workshops, such as those referenced throughout this book, and through mentorship.

We can integrate many ways of knowing by working with others that have different training and starting assumptions. They can help us or even challenge us to think outside our own boxes or even burn the box (Alphonse, 2009).

CHAPTER 21. Connecting through ritual.

There are some well-developed, effective rituals and ceremonies that are specifically aimed at connecting with the land. Other traditional ceremonies can be modified to incorporate some of the techniques discussed in the book to make them better avenues for connecting strongly with nature. Also, new rituals and ceremonies can be created to help us work with nature in different ways or add to our toolbox of techniques.

Native American pipe ceremonies are great for plugging in to the spirit world. During the unwrapping of the pipes, especially if many pipes are present, I feel the energy come into the area – the spirit animals and ancestors involved with those pipes are joining us. The smoking may appear casual, and the spirits are there with us. We are communing with them. By smoking the pipe, we interact with modern nature spirits and ancestral nature spirits (two leggeds, four leggeds, winged, plant, stone, and more) including the Tobacco Spirit.

T21.1. Council of All Beings.
The "Council of All Beings" is a soul moving/perspective changing/mind expanding ritual technique that involves playing the role of specific creatures or beings of nature in a meeting of the minds (Fleming and Macy, 1988). Channeling and/or speaking for a specific nature entity or energy gets us closer to empathizing and being one with that entity or energy. The experience of representing a nature being may be similar to acting in the theater, may resemble channeling or evocation in religious ceremonies, and/or may be completely unique. The experience can vary based on the way that you engage with the exercise as well as vary with the entities and energies that are involved. The first time I participated in one of these ceremonies was at Full Circle Farm in Pennsylvania. I played the role of the Potomac River and spoke for it in the council. The experience combined an empathic connection with the river with my intellectual understanding of the river. I looked at the river in a new way, having different imagery in my mind's eye visualizations and memories of the Potomac. I internalized the river's identity and concerns in a new and different way.

The Council of All Beings involves activities and preparations that transform us into the role of a nature being or aspect and then involves speaking for that aspect/being. As preparation for the incorporation of the Council of All Beings into a Druid ceremony at Allen's creek, members of Black Bear Grove journeyed as a group to meet the Allen's Creek Goddess and also did personal work to track toward the ceremony. For my personal preparation, I journeyed and communed with the spirits (both physical site wandering and shamanic journey) and I made a blue meandering pullover stole that I put on to become the creek. Others in the group made more elaborate costumes. Another group did a mask-making session before another Council of All Beings event, giving me a chance to work with goat energy as I made and donned my mask.

During two different years, as part of the Connecting with the Land Workshop Series, a Council of All Beings ceremony served as the final installment of a sequence of events aimed at building relationships with nature allies. During the first event in the sequence, we did the classic journey to meet nature spirit allies. The second event allowed us to deepen our relationships with nature allies. During the third event, we made costumes and masks, then we channeled or otherwise communed with our nature allies, and then the nature beings communicated with each other in a council.

Reverence for nature is appropriate for many types of ritual and ceremony. Gestures of deference, praise, and respect for nature can be inserted into your ceremonies, personal routines, work routines, and community role(s). Personal and group ritual can be tailored to help you weave nature into your personal practice and can work hand in hand with relationships with guiding spirits. Reverence and respect can be part of and inspire environmental service. Dialogue with nature beings and environmental service can be done regularly.

A number of techniques can be used to prepare for a ceremony aimed at getting a group more in touch with nature. For example, during the weekend before a 2004 spring equinox celebration, I strolled along a ridgetop and down into a valley in Morgan-Monroe State Forest and noticed wildflowers coming up along the east and northeast facing valley slopes. The harbinger of spring was blooming, cut leaved toothwort leaves and flower buds were present, and spring beauty leaves had come up. The beauty of spring was easy to see and inspired good ritual work. I advocate preparing for ceremonies with an extensive dialogue with the land. I get good results when I ask for guidance, and this correlation seems to hold for others as well.

During the hours leading up to a spring equinox ceremony, members of Black Bear Grove did a litter clean up. During the ceremony, offerings were given to the local spirits. After the ceremony, some of the celebrants slept out under the night sky. The group connected with the land in multiple ways on the journey associated with the ceremony. The process facilitated deep connection while the blooming wildflowers and budding trees added levity.

Asking for fire during ceremonies can be another important dialogue to have with both local and archetypal entities and energies. Considerations and relationships are similar to those discussed in Chapter 18. The dialogue related to building a fire for survival also applies to one built for a ceremony. Asking for permission and guidance are both particularly important.

Druid ceremonies designate a birch priest (referring to the ability of birch bark to hold a flame – a natural combination of tinder and kindling), someone devoted to building and working with the ritual fire. The role of fire keeper is also very important in sweat lodge ceremonies.

Setting up altars and shrines in ceremonial space at outdoor or indoor sites is quality devotional time, which helps to deepen relationships with nature beings. Shrines can be set up temporarily for a ceremony or can be part of an established ceremonial site. The fairy shrine at Wisteria and shrines at Lothlorien Nature Sanctuary as well as the altars and statues in the Nemeton and Runestead at the Brushwood Folklore Center are the evolving result of devotion from many people over time. Nature objects can be included on our personal altars and can help us plug into nature, even while indoors. Special rocks and crystals, plants, and pieces of driftwood can all invoke memories or allow us to journey with the nature spirit present in the object. In addition, we can wear nature's materials as talismans or for protection, or other magical intent (see Chapter 12 for some of the correspondences that might be involved in nature magic). Energy work, art, prayers, song, meditation, shamanic practices, and other techniques mentioned in previous chapters are often incorporated into group ceremonies as well as personal practice.

Parts of traditional style rituals are designed to honor nature spirits in general (e.g., nature spirit invocation in Ár nDraíocht Féin ritual), spirits associated with certain directions (e.g., honoring directions in Native American ceremonies or calling quarters in Wicca and eclectic Neopagan traditions), or other specific spirits (e.g., stone people and plant spirits invoked in ceremonies at the Temple of Sophia in Massachusetts). A variety of cultural lenses may influence the language used (names for beings include: fairies, land wights, stone people, star people, nature spirits, elementals, and land spirits). Specific elementals and animal spirits are associated with the directions. For example, a generalized Native American set of correspondences associates the Eagle with the east, Coyote with the south, Bear with the west, and White Buffalo with the north. Honoring the directions, as well as other ritual parts, can be focused to help us connect locally with nature around our ritual sites or to foster general, overarching connections that broaden our sense of nature.

T21.2. Invoke nature spirits in ceremony.
Nature spirits can be invoked in many ways. When I am called to invoke them in ceremony, I like to ask the spirits how they want to be invoked and listen to what they tell me. I usually have some information emerge in my consciousness as I meditate at the site before the ceremony. Walking circles can allow insights to come in as well.

In cases where it is difficult to plug in enough to listen to nature's input or if the information is not flowing for some other reason, a good backup plan is to go with what is observed at the ceremony site and honor those aspects of nature. An invocation at a spring equinox celebration was based on what I observed near the site:

> Cut leaved toothwort and cress blooming at the bottom of the hollow. Buds swelling on the trees. Spring coming. You are waking up after the winter. Nature spirits! Hail and welcome!

Sometimes the invocation can relate to conditions during the ceremony and challenges members of the group may be experiencing. The following is an approximation of a winter nature spirit invocation:

> Cool, chilling, biting air.
> Tentative winter Sun shedding diffuse light on a desolate landscape.
> Blanketing clouds.
> Invading clouds.

Dormant life.
Sleeping trees.
Stark outlines of life.
We conduct a rite among you.
Join us as we try to join you.

While communicating with the land at Brushwood Folklore Center in summer 2004, I received messages to add more to the nature spirit invocation that I was asked to do for the Starwood opening circle. The following is an approximation of the words used:

Spirits of nature. Spirits of this land.
Groundwater moving through the soil into lake and stream.
Blood flowing through our veins.
Bedrock beneath the soil.
Bones give shape to our bodies.
The hawthorn growing between the two fields, and maples of the Fairy Woods.
Clover and grasses of this field.
Willow and milkweed around the lake.
Black cherry and club moss.
And the creatures who dwell within our sacred grove.
We call out to all of you spirits of this land.
We wish to dwell among you during the Starwood Festival.
We wish to do this in a way that honors you.
Guide us to live in balance with you here on these hills and in this valley.
We open our hearts and minds to you.

We were on high open ground so the celebrants could follow with their eyes the journey through the landscape that was invoked along with the nature spirits. The movement kept the longish invocation palatable.

Here is an example of a rock and mineral invocation done in the "stone people" slot at the Goddess Mountain Summer Solstice of 2013:

Now it is time to honor rock and mineral spirits. Crystalline rock below the soil, forming the core of this mountain, holding our ritual space in place. You are the reason our blood is red, you provide taste to our drinking water. Rock and mineral spirits! Hail and welcome!

And here is the thanking at the end of the ceremony:

Rock. Bedrock of the mountain. Bits of rock that make up the soil. Cobbles and pebbles in the local streams. You are among us. Let us see if we can tune our consciousness toward you and vibrate in a way that allows us to converse with you. May we all be at peace. Hail and farewell.

T21.3. Design and enact ceremonies in honor of nature entities and energies.
Some ceremonies are held to honor nature in a big picture sense. Others focus on

specific aspects of nature. And others do intensive work with local processes and beings. Ceremonies can be designed to specifically work with local nature entities and energies (including nature spirits). The following are examples that involve the adaptation of the Ár nDraíocht Féin (ADF) ritual style to work with local beings:

- Mugwort Grove fall equinox celebration held along the shoreline of the northern part of the Chesapeake Bay in 1999. The background given and outline followed by this ceremony/ritual were as follows:

BACKGROUND
One purpose of this fall equinox ritual is to honor local deities using our understanding of them and in our way. So, the deities chosen were the spirit/energy of the wind, the Susquehanna River, the Chesapeake Bay, and the woods.

One way of getting in tune with these gods is to consider how the Native Americans that lived around here had honored their particular deities and spirits. Below is a discussion of Native American lore associated with parts of our ritual.

Tidbits for the Story of the Season
The Native American tribes of the area honored their specific corn gods/goddesses with offerings from various stages of their harvest. At this time of year they were likely starting to prepare for winter and wanting to affirm plenty of game to hunt in the coming months. The Piscataway tribe located between the Potomac and Patapsco rivers in Maryland had honored a "Great Spirit" that they called Manito (In literature for other tribes this god is spelled "Manitou") (Manakee, 1959; Hultkrantz, 1979). They honored him at the harvest and he is thought to be their equivalent of the corn goddesses and gods that were broadly honored for land fertility.

Gatekeeper – Goddess of the Susquehanna
The Susquehannocks were a tribe located along the Susquehanna River. We will be holding ritual in what was part of their territory (Manakee, 1959). They may have had a mother goddess figure as their corn goddess, because they were loosely associated with the Iroquois Confederacy. We are invoking the Goddess of the Susquehanna as our gate keeper, partly because we cross the Susquehanna in our trek to the park and partly because the Susquehannocks were known as extraordinarily large and fierce (Ferguson, 1941) – so a river goddess of their lands would be a good guard of the gates.

Bard – Spirits of the Winds
Native Americans honored spirits of air in the form of birds. I thought it would be appropriate to invoke Spirits of the Winds to provide us with the proper amount of breath (wind) to complete our ritual.

Patron – Woodland God/Forest Spirit
Many Native Americans have honored forest spirits. The Susquehannock were likely to do so, due to their affinity for the hunt, but I didn't find a name for a Susquehannock woodland deity. This god could be considered a local Cernunnos.

Patron – God of the Chesapeake
Algonkin peoples (the Piscataway and Delaware were two local tribes that were of the Algonkin linguistic stock) and other Native American tribes seem to have honored water spirits having the forms of great serpents or water snakes (Hultkrantz, 1979).

RITUAL OUTLINE
1. Kindle fire and set up site
2. Pre-ritual briefing
3. Musical signal to process to sigil site
4. Processional chant
5. Smudge when entering ritual site
6. Opening prayer and offering to the Earth Mother
7. Unity chant
8. Invite bardic assistance (Spirits of the Winds)
9. Grove meditation (tree meditation)
10. Story of the season and ritual statement of purpose
11. Outsider offering
12. Establish Sacred Center
13. Invite Gate Keeper (Goddess of the Susquehanna; European approximation – Irish river goddess "Boann") and open the gates
14. Invite three kindreds: nature spirits, ancestors, and deities
15. Invite Patron Power 1 (God of Eastern N. American Woodlands; European approximation – Cernunnos)
16. Invite Patron Power 2 (God of the Chesapeake Bay; European approximation – Manannan mac Lir)
17. Praise offerings and final blessing
18. Seek interpretive omen
19. Hallowing & passing of the Waters of Life
20. Formal working
21. Thanks to the God of the Chesapeake
22. Thanks to the God of the Forest
23. Thanks to the kindreds
24. Close the gates and thank the Goddess of the Susquehanna
25. Thank the Spirits of the Winds for their bardic assistance
26. Undo the tree meditation
27. End

Modified from the event's handout text included in Davis (2004).

- Mugwort Grove spring equinox ceremony at Pohick Bay Regional Park along the Potomac River in which bird spirits, a woodland deity, and a river goddess were invoked. Praising water flow through the landscape was a dominant theme, and appropriately, it poured rain during the whole ceremony.
- Fall equinox along Allen's Creek. The Druids of Black Bear Grove worked with a guardian oak, the Allen's Creek Goddess, as well as beings channeled by participants.

These ceremonies are examples of efforts to connect with local spirits by ADF members. Other ADF groves have employed a variety of techniques to develop relationships with local river goddesses and other nature spirits. Ellison (2003) provides an account of some of these efforts and tips for developing relationships with the land.

Groups conducting ceremonies of diverse traditions and styles can supplement or even complement theological, archetypal, or therapeutic work with engagement with local land spirits, energies, or other aspects of nature. The locals often appreciate the effort.

Most of the events of the Connecting with the Land Workshop Series are both workshops and ceremonies. Our ceremonial work has involved singing and dancing with trees, engaging with land energies, mountain alchemy, various kinds of work with rivers, conversations and communion with the bedrock, and multidimensional interactions with ecosystems. Each event is customized to synergize with the human participants, location, nature entities, and nature energies.

CHAPTER 22. Group "Connecting with the Land" exercises.

Appalachian Mountains
Ridges of strong quartz sandstone
Long peaceful hollows
Carved as water penetrates weaker rocks
Druids
Naturalists
Flow with the contours of the land
Move among the nature spirits
Focusing in one place
Feeling the energies and essence
Then focusing in another
$\qquad$ Adam Davis, 2002

The connecting techniques in this book have come to me through mentors in many traditions, work as a Naturalist and geologist, various workshops and personal study, group and solo shamanic journeys, my personal practice, group ceremonies of many traditions, work with Druid groups and ceremony, and communications with many different landscapes and aspects of nature over the course of my life. I enjoy collaborating with others to learn new ways to connect, and I encourage you to be open to learning from multiple teachers as well. Remember, "beginner's mind". Ellison (2003) and Cornett (1988) are examples of excellent, worthwhile workshops for working with nature spirits. Attending Cornett's workshop early in the new millennium was helpful for me, because it reinforced the importance of asking permission and maintaining a dialogue with natural communities. These remain critical aspects of my practice today.

The goal of the "Connecting with the Land Workshop Series", which I have been facilitating since 1998, is to help integrate many different connecting styles and to serve participants based on their unique backgrounds. Keeping with this goal, connecting with the land group exercises that I facilitate vary based on the participants. The idea is to allow the character of the land and the chemistry of the group to influence the flow of these flexible, dynamic workshops. Custom work with themes, the place, and the folks that attend gives the workshops and ceremonies in this series their unique character. Folks can also get support in enhancing their relationships with the natural world through offerings from other facilitators whose work may be known as nature mindfulness, forest bathing, deep ecology, nature spirituality, plant spirit medicine, water ceremonies, nature connection, and/or other names.

Varieties of workshops in the Connecting with the Land Workshop Series include generally connecting with nature at a place and deepening relationships with aspects of nature, connecting with water flow and water bodies, mountain alchemy, working with nature allies for emotional and physical wellness, connecting with rocks and minerals, communicating with and learning from trees, environmental memorial services, cultivating relationships with nature allies, giving praise and thanks to nature entities and energies, exploring diverse nature connection techniques, working with energies of the landscape, environmental service support, land stewardship, conservation, and more.

The general connecting with nature workshop variety often involves a hello to local nature entities and energies, followed by a sharing circle and brief talk about connecting with the land techniques, followed by the main work – part guided visualization and part self-directed exploration, and closing with another sharing circle and a thank you to the nature entities and energies. I give an introductory spiel at the beginning, taking us from practical connections to connections we may mark as especially sacred. An initial sharing circle allows celebrants to describe some of the ways that they are connected as well as specific techniques they use to plug in on a spiritual level. During a technique focused discussion period, and/or technique discussions and demonstrations spread throughout the workshop, I work to ensure that all in attendance have an appropriate technique to work with before we move on from the introductory and preparatory phase. Protection invocation and cleansing, done near the beginning, are important traditional parts of this kind of workshop as well as all the workshops of the Connecting with the Land Workshop Series. After our preparatory work, there may be a walk from the initial gathering point to the place where we reach deeper. The walk allows for discussion and meditation which help us to begin to connect with the area. Once at our focus site, we may engage in a visualization or use another technique for plugging in to the energies. Then we move into personal work/journeys which may use techniques discussed earlier and/or others. A closing sharing circle allows celebrants to relate impressions, thoughts, feelings, and/or catharses that they experienced through the work. Sometimes we move to a second location and explore its energy, sensing and comparing the differences with the first site. Rich discussions about the character of places in the landscape typically follow. Giving thanks to nature entities and energies, including our protectors and sources of inspiration, is a critical part of the closing of the workshop and ceremonial space.

Example descriptions and outlines of past workshops include:

- Description of a workshop held at the Starwood Festival in 2022: Multidimensional Nature Awareness
  > You are invited to join us for an exploration of diverse ways of connecting with nature. We will spend time observing nature's beauty and power, and then we will deepen our awareness with meditative techniques. After becoming aware of magical aspects of the landscape, we will have opportunities to enrich our engagement with the natural world through communications with nature entities and energies, energy exchange, and trancework. After the scheduled part of the workshop, facilitator Adam Davis will be available for discussion and exploration of more dimensions of nature awareness.

- Mount Tom, 10/3/2012, outline:
  1. Introduction about connectedness.

2. Sharing ways that we connect.
3. Ensuring that everyone has a new technique to work with.
4. Saying hello – getting into the right frame of mind [our chance to contact the essence(s) of the area, to introduce ourselves, and to begin to listen to the wisdom of the place].
5. Getting present on the walk in to the site – possibly with a walking meditation.
6. Seeking personal guides for journeying.
7. Bowing and giving offerings to a guardian oak and witch hazel.
8. Bowing when entering the site.
9. Guided visualization down into the Earth, then along the surface, up through canopy, and up the mountain side.
10. Solo exploration.
11. Sharing circle.
12. Chant.
13. Giving thanks.

- Rites of Spring 2011 description:
  "Connecting with the Land – In this workshop, we will connect with a sacred space within the landscape of the Berkshires. We will have a chance to deepen our relationships with nature by employing ritual and meditation techniques to explore spirit energies and natural forces of the land" (EarthSpirit, 2011).

- Description in the program of the 3rd Annual Simply Living Fair, Bloomington, IN, November 2008:
  "Exploring Connections with the Land – An interactive and experiential exploration of our sensual, philosophical, and spiritual relationships with our environment. Participants will work with new techniques for exploring and reflecting upon their relationships to nature" (Coleman et al., 2008).

These workshops aspire to give each participant a new technique, so with some groups meeting this goal requires more up front discussion and demonstration of techniques than with other groups. For more accounts and pictures of past workshops as well as announcements of upcoming events please see the Facebook Page of the workshop series – Connecting with the Land (2013).

I encourage dialogue with various entities and energies of nature throughout these workshops. I personally engage in conversations with nature before, during, and after events. I check with the land before I lead a workshop in a particular place or region. I ask nature beings and land energies what they want me to teach in the workshop. What do they want in the ceremony? What kinds of offerings do they like or are appropriate for the occasion at hand? When I do this sort of check in with nature, I often get inspirations regarding what to emphasize and how to conduct the workshop or class. For example, before the Connecting with the Land workshop on Mt. Tom in the fall of 2012, the omen was to work with the trees. Asking for permission is a key part of the dialogue before the workshop. Consent and respect is important.

The variety in past workshop experiences was influenced by the nature and state of the participants as well as the energies of the locations. Example groups and types of experiences have included Druids checking out water flow patterns and hugging trees together, college students meditating along a creek, people from diverse walks of life connecting with nature entities and energies of a mature forest, nature lovers singing and dancing with trees, folks versed in shamanic techniques engaging with a North Woods wetland via multiple pathways and dimensions, folks of diverse traditions meditating and flowing with the river, community organizers and environmentalists connecting with nature in an inner city setting, facilitators and clergy of diverse traditions finding the next techniques and messages for incorporating nature connection work into their practices and teachings, folks receiving therapy and vision on transformational mountain journeys, deep ecologists and eclectic animists wandering the landscape of gatherings and festivals, and environmentally minded folks communing with a picturesque ridgetop site as part of a sustainability fair.

During talking stick portions of workshops, which often occur after a combined group and solo journey, participants have shared many interesting experiences. Some attendees stated that they never before sat quietly in a place in nature. They had never done a meditative activity or communed with nature before, and were grateful to be opened to the possibilities. Others were finding new phenomena and insights based on the unique energies of the place and the perspectives they brought. Participants can get greater clarity and new revelations about their experiences as they hear others talk. Shared impressions and visions are not uncommon in these group exercises.

Here are some reflections/reports from specific past events:
- Workshops at the Bloomington Simply Living Fair given in two different years were completely different. One was on a nose landform of the landscape in a mature forest. The other was near a tree in an urban setting. We deepened in further to a connection with the nose forest, but we covered more techniques in an intellectual fashion in the more urban setting.
- For multiple years at the Free Spirit Gathering, the work focused on connecting with the beings present. Seeing a young eagle along the banks of the Susquehanna was quite mystical. Praises given to trees, shrubs, rock, and soil were very moving.
- An intuitive participant heard the echoes of the kids swinging from the "Triple Oak" at Our Haven Nature Sanctuary in French Lick, IN. Another felt that the tree missed having children play among its branches.
- A participant at an exercise in the Silver Woods of the Brushwood Folklore Center in western New York State showed me a new way to journey through the landscape by the way that she linked her intuition with the land.
- Shamanically moving down through a swallow hole in Spring Mill State Park happened very naturally for members of the Druid group called Black Bear

Grove. This group also had a very rewarding physical journey combined with shamanic and energy work in the Jordan River watershed, intuitively coming together in a circle around a giant bur oak in Dunn Meadow in Bloomington, IN.

- At an exercise in Northampton, MA, a spirit picked the pocket of a participant and took an important personal item so that she was compelled to go back to find it later. She was then called to sit and meditate again and then reminded to regularly make time to deepen with nature.
- At an ad hoc exercise in Bloomington, IN, a woman realized that she can use her intuition and psychic ability, which she had used during work with humans, while interacting with trees. She realized she could dialogue with trees and that sometimes trees don't want human interaction.
- In a workshop in the Berkshires along the Appalachian Trail, having heard me mention the technique of the Council of All Beings, a man decided to connect with the entire council rather than play the role of one particular nature being. He obtained and shared deep, textured wisdom regarding working with nature in a more balanced way.
- At a gathering in Prince William Forest Park, a co-facilitated workshop combined some rich background about the place with our experiential exercise. Sitting on a stream bar in the creek, some connected with the essence of the local land and others had contemplative experiences related to plugging into bigger picture patterns and ancestral connections.
- An ad hoc exercise near Shade Gap, PA, in the fall of 2000 was particularly rich because it involved comparing two locations. The exercise featured time to deepen at each location, and it involved participants who all had a rich personal practice of connecting with the land. The exercise was facilitated by the Archdruid of a Druid order. The sharing circle results reflected the richness and depth that can come from a gathering of multidimensional Naturalists. The feelings and sense of the site and type of magic that could be done were compared between the two locations. Participants commented on the stark and desolate nature of the first site, and they indicated a variety of sensations related to more stability and comfort at the second site. An overall enchantment and playful energies were perceived at the second location, and two of the participants were playing with the fairy folk who dwelled there (Dobhran et al., 2002). This exercise was very influential in the development of the connecting with the land exercises that I facilitate. Hail the essence and residents of Full Circle Farm for hosting us and hail the folks who did the work!

To give more of a sense of how group exercises can go, I am including the following modified excerpt from my journal that was recorded two days after a connecting exercise conducted on December 1, 2005, in southern Indiana.

Three of us (a woman and two men, including myself) did a connecting with the land exercise on a broad ridgetop in southern Indiana. I was not all that "plugged in" and had felt resistance to us doing the work. I envisioned problems after I borrowed a friend's car and then the road was blocked off on the way out to the site. But, we made it out. A couple of us in the group picked up on the differences between the old natural order of the mature forest of the valley that we walked through on the way to the site and the striving young forest of an abandoned agricultural field on the ridgetop. Once we sat in the middle of the young forest, the woman saw native ancestors talking about the paths being the same but that the modern inhabitants don't know where they are. The other man in the group professed to not connecting all that well, but mentioned noticing the snow that fell on us as we sat and that the raven flying overhead was an omen. I saw a hooded man moving in when my eyes were closed – it was a presence that came in – it may have been associated with the raven and so I considered that it might be one of Odin's ravens (Thought). I felt like the message to me was that I was thinking too much and trying to force my nature connection. I noticed all the dead herbs blowing in the wind, the snow, and a diffuse light. I also saw a connected woman – part of the place. The woman in the group saw (with her eyes open) the/a hooded figure swoop down. She also had cedars show her their young one – showing her the cycle of fertility and oneness. She received the message of death, but also of rebirth. She also saw a couple in a corn field. I received a message to get more meditation into my daily practice.

The journey within a journey within our oneness of this experience brings tears of joy to my eyes as I write about it, and as I relive it. We were doing timeless, divine work. The message about the pathways has stuck with me ever since – a constant source of inspiration to find and honor the current and old pathways of many beings through the landscape.

Figure 22.1. Connecting with the land exercise in southern Indiana in late fall 2005.
(Kalavaris, 2013)

More workshop reflections, organized by workshop type, can be found on the
Connecting with the Land Workshop Series website accessible via
https://www.landsolution.com/connectingwiththeland.html (URL confirmed on
6/21/2023).

CHAPTER 23. Combining techniques.

At times, we may be able to fully realize the depth of our nature connections with a single technique of this book. On other occasions, it may take multiple methods.

T23.1. Employ many ways of knowing and/or multiple techniques at the same time and in various sequences.
There is value in stringing together multiple techniques. One technique can lead to another. Used in sequences, these methods can build upon one another, creating the deepening effect discussed in Chapter 3. A combination of techniques can get us present, into the moment, plugged in, connected, and into realizing that we are the place.

One approach involves authentically (intuitively) shifting through a series of techniques, like shifting gears when driving an automobile. You can let the land guide you, communing and communicating with nature entities and energies as you go. This can be a great way to explore the sacredness of the land and a place (see Chapter 9).

Sometimes we learn the value of multiple techniques by being in the right place at the right time and through help from others. When I walked back into a thicket for my first Druid ceremony, a woman was there and she sang:

        Ancient Mother   …   I hear you calling
        Ancient Mother   …   I hear your song
        Ancient Mother   …   I feel your laughter
        Ancient Mother   …   I taste your tears
                        Traditional Earth Mother Chant

My soul was instantly humming with her and that space. The short bushwhack, the chant, and the start of the ceremony are emblazoned into my memory.

Another way that use of multiple connecting methods has deepened my practice has been through my work with trees over the years. Knowing tree characteristics feeds, and is fed by, knowledge of the Earth System and smaller regional ecosystems. Knowing through empiricism and scholarship can feed a sense of companionship and dialogue with specific trees. Trees become friends. Then, seeing them can be like seeing familiar human faces (like seeing people you know).

Simple physical observations can be a good starting point for these multi-method journeys. Observations can show us nature's diversity and can help us experience the richness of Earth's ecosystems. Several of my former geology students have commented that they see much more variety in the rock exposures along roadways than they did in the past. Some reported having driven by bedrock exposures many times over decades of their lives without really looking at the rocks. Taking time to make observations opened doors for them.

Detailed understanding of the characteristics of an area can also help with association magic, symbology, metaphor, and other ways to find inspiration. If you can recognize a vulture versus a red tailed hawk versus a bald eagle, you can accurately tap into cultural symbolism, share stories with Naturalists, and add a variety of other potential layers to your experience. Identification can support multidisciplinary exploration of many nature phenomena.

Mixing archetypal and metaphorical musings with physical sensations can be rich. We can combine philosophical, artistic, "all senses", and shamanic ways of connecting. Smell the ocean floor.

Employing meditative or artistic connection techniques at places that have been empirically studied can be very rewarding. Differences in place described from a scientific or Naturalist perspective can relate to differences in place felt deeply on a personal level. For example, "Connecting with the Land" workshop participants felt an old natural order while walking through a mature forest ecosystem in contrast to the young, striving, discontented energy that they noticed after arriving at the main workshop site, which was located in a successional abandoned agricultural field.

Group work that combines techniques often benefits from specific rewards of the multiple methods and is enriched by diverse perspectives in the group. We can achieve unique connecting with the land experiences through freeform collaborations guided by the intuitive, timely contributions of each member. We play off each other.

Personal and group ritual work can be optimized by combining it with dialogue and authentic wandering methods, because these exploratory methods help us discover how the character of a particular place influences the outcomes of work conducted there. Accounting for the effects of the land elevates the chance of success of prayers, rituals, ceremonies, and various magical workings. For example, if you are facilitating a two powers visualization to get people grounded and in touch with the ritual location, you could talk the celebrants through images of generic soil and bedrock or you could utilize knowledge of the local geology when facilitating the visualization. Which do you think I would recommend? Is it respectful to the local flora, fauna, rock, and soil to do spiritual connection exercises with different flora, fauna, rock, and soil without acknowledging the locals? No! Converse with and honor the locals!

The value of using many methods, keeping an open mind, and "going with the flow" cannot be overstated. Occupying multiple states of consciousness and being at the same time (multivalency) can be extremely valuable. Sometimes I feel like I am cascading through many layers and many lenses. Nature is leading me. The energy flows of the landscape are shaping me. The essence of place permeates my body.

CHAPTER 24. Conclusion.

"One is the beginning" Spock

T24.1. Believe with soul in oneness with the Earth, and in your part in the Earth System.
An intellectual understanding of connectedness is a step along the path of realizing our connectedness with the land. We can go further, engaging our energy and spirit in a deeper way through believing oneness in a faith-based way and/or feeling it in our hearts and souls. The techniques in this book can help facilitate this belief. Let us chant:

> Earth my body
> Water my blood
> Air my breath and
> Fire my spirit

This book has been about cultivating and realizing deeper connections with land, nature, and environment. It is about personal growth. It advocates holistic connectedness with Earth. The techniques in this book are useful in developing diverse connections with nature, and I encourage using as many as feel appropriate to you. Ideally, each of us will experience unique and personal ways of connecting. I hope you are able to go to many depths and taste many flavors of nature relationships.

Multifaceted connections with nature and environment can help us maintain or improve our quality of life, and can help us become positive voices in shaping community decisions. Now is a time to be mindful about our connectedness and to take action to deal with changes that humans have brought to the Earth System. We are faced with increased flood and storm impacts; resource scarcity, degradation, and resulting conflicts; and pollution of soil, water, and air. Awareness and understanding of cause and effect in the Earth System or individual ecosystems (and theoretically sound planning that could result) can be enhanced by cultivating spiritual nature connections. Solutions are revealed through Earth knowledge.

Spiritual connections with nature are central to our wellbeing. We can be aware, smart, and respectful in our work with the land; and we can support solutions to environmental and other societal problems. Nurturing relationships with nature is similar to networking in other aspects of our communities. These nature energies, forces, and beings are our neighbors. Communicating and working with the land is part of our role in the community and as planetary citizens.

Technique	Page
T18.15. Ramp up and practice survival skills.	119
T19.1. Conduct clean-ups.	122
T19.2. Prevent the spread of invasive species.	122
T19.3. Participate in invasive species pulls.	122
T19.4. Practice and support land conservation.	123
T19.5. Volunteer with watershed advocacy groups.	123
T19.6. Monitor logging, mining, and drilling companies.	123
T19.7. Be an active voice in natural resource management and environmental policy.	123
T19.8. Support efficient salvage and waste management practices, and report illegal dumping.	123
T19.9. Reduce, reuse, recycle.	123
T19.10. Make smart personal choices to support sustainability.	123
T19.11. Avoid using pesticides and chemical fertilizers.	123
T19.12. Support societal efforts that encourage sustainability.	124
T19.13. Be an environmental advocate.	124
T19.14. Engage in environmental activism.	124
T19.15. Commit to land stewardship.	124
T21.1. Council of All Beings.	127
T21.2. Invoke nature spirits in ceremony.	129
T21.3. Design and enact ceremonies in honor of nature entities and energies.	130
T23.1. Employ many ways of knowing and/or multiple techniques at the same time and in various sequences.	141
T24.1. Believe with soul in oneness with the Earth, and in your part in the Earth System.	143

GLOSSARY

Ár nDraíocht Féin (ADF) – Gaelic for "Our Own Druidry" and the name of an international Druid order founded by P. E. Isaac Bonewits.

Aura – Energy field associated with beings. Can be detected by eye, felt by hands, or sensed through general intuition.

Basic Visualization Technique – Creating a visual sequence or journey in the mind's eye.

Bedrock – Rock type and specific rock unit of the Earth's crust that is immediately below a particular geographic place and/or is at the Earth's surface in that place or area (e.g., the bedrock of much of the Bloomington campus of Indiana University is a rock unit called the "Salem Limestone").

Beginner's mind – A mindset conducive to sensing patterns and flows of energy.

Black Bear Grove – A congregation of Ár nDraíocht Féin.

Chakras – Energy centers in the body described and used traditionally by Vedic and Hindu religions including Yoga practices, and by New Age healers.

Cosmology – An understanding and structure of the cosmos of a particular religion.

Druids – Priests, healers, and wise people of Celtic tribal culture, and members of various subsequent revivals inspired by this cultural element including modern "Neodruids".

Ecological footprint – The total environmental impact from a person or enterprise.

Energy – Power potential. Feeling/vibration associated with states of being.

Energy patterns – Variations in energy through space and time.

Hollows – Valleys.

Journeying – Technique for spirit travel regardless of what the physical body is doing.

Karst terrain – Landscape with sinkholes and caves developed by weathering of limestone over time.

Ley line – 1. Line that can be envisioned across the surface of the Earth to connect specific cultural features. 2. Line of power identified on or near the surface of the Earth which is commonly multiple kilometers long, although it may be shorter.

Magic – 1. Mystical and/or wondrous happenings. 2. The art of working with energy patterns or states of being with intent to change them or change perceptions of them.

Metaphysical – Beyond the physical. Refers to properties useful in magic and energy work.

Mudras – Hand postures that have specific metaphysical properties and power.

Multivalent – Act of being in or potential to be in multiple states of being simultaneously.

Neopagans – Modern polytheists, pantheists, and dualtheists of many traditions not including continuous traditions of thousands of years (such as Lakota, Hindu, or Yoruba).

New Age – A range of philosophies and practices including those regarded as alternative medicine, occult, metaphysical, paranormal, and spiritualist.

Nexus – Collection of many energy patterns sometimes referring to a generative collaboration or synergy (e.g., a causal nexus).

Noses – Places where upland juts out from along a ridge or at the end of a ridge.

Power – Energy that can be or is channeled for spiritual or magical work.

Power spot – Point in the landscape that has a concentration of energy.

Reiki – Healing tradition involving healing through energy transfer through the hands.

Shamans – In diverse past and present cultures, "healer-priests who are the chief intermediaries between human beings and the sacred world" (Cooper, 1993).

Shamanic – Related to methods and practices used by shamans.

Shamanic State of Consciousness – A state of mind, emotion, and overall awareness conducive to journeying.

Shoulder – Area between the flat top of a ridge and the steep slopes on the sides.

Spirit – 1. Sacred essence. 2. A being without an easily observable physical form. 3. An observed and/or not observed energy and/or entity.

Spiritual – Of the essence(s) of beings or energies and the reverence of it/them.

Spiritual practice – Activities specifically intended to nourish the spirit.

Spring – Place where groundwater comes out of the ground and begins a creek.

State of consciousness – State of mind, emotion(s), and overall awareness.

Swallow hole – Sinkhole that a stream flows into.

Topographic relief – Difference in elevation between high and low points in the landscape.

Visualization – Following sequences of images with the mind's eye. Similar to dreaming.

World Tree – 1. Symbolic tree that connects aspects of religious cosmologies. 2. Central pillar or axis that unites the worlds of the cosmos (Willis, 1993b).

REFERENCES

Some of the web page URLs that were included in the first edition were verified, updated, or removed during the 2021 to 2023 editing period for this second edition. In cases where a URL is included in a reference listing, the date of last access is included in brackets after the URL.

Abbey, E., In *Earth Prayers From Around The World: 365 Prayers, Poems, and Invocations For Honoring The Earth*. Elizabeth Roberts and Elias Amidon Eds., 1991, HarperCollins Publishers, New York, NY.

Abbey, E., 1975, *The Monkey Wrench Gang*. Lippincott Williams & Wilkins, Philadelphia, PA.

ACE, 2022, Starwood 2022. The Starwood Festival. Association for Consciousness Exploration.

Aelwyd, A., Personal communication.

Aguado, E., Burt, J.E., 2010, *Understanding weather and climate*. Fifth Edition. Prentice Hall, NY.

Alphonse, M.A., 2009, Burn the Box. Workshop. Bloomington, IN.

American Meteorological Society, 2012, *Glossary of Meteorology*.

Ancient-Wisdom, 2013, Ley-lines. URL: http://www.ancient-wisdom.com/leylines.htm [accessed in 2013].

Andrews, T., 1993, *Animal Speak: The Spiritual & Magical Powers of Creatures Great & Small*. Llewellyn Publications, Woodbury, MN.

Ár nDraíocht Féin, 2013. ADF Core Order of Ritual. URL: http://www.adf.org/rituals/explanations/core-order.html [accessed in 2013].

The Backwoodsman Magazine. URL: http://backwoodsmanmag.com/ [accessed in 2023].

Beth and Zeeb, 2013, Feywood. URL: https://www.facebook.com/Feywood/ [accessed in 2013].

Bonewits, P.E.I., Lady Liberty Ritual. Sacred Space Conference. Timonium, MD.

Bonewits, P.E.I., 1971, *Real Magic*. Samuel Weiser, Inc., York Beach, ME.

Brennan, B.A., 1987, *Hands of Light: A Guide to Healing Through the Human Energy Field*. Bantam Books, New York, NY.

Brown, T.Jr., 1985, *Tom Brown's Guide to Wild Edible and Medicinal Plants*. The Berkley Publishing Group, New York, NY.

Callenbach, E., 1975, *Ecotopia: The Notebooks and Reports of William Weston*, Random House, New York, NY.

Carr-Gomm, P., Carr-Gomm, S., Worthington, B., 1995, *The Druid Animal Oracle*. Touchstone Books, New York, NY.

Carson, R., 1962, *Silent Spring*. Houghton Mifflin, Boston, MA.

Casamira, T., 2013, Personal communication. Amethyst Brook, MA.

Cerier, L., 2013. The Organic Gourmet. URL: http://www.lesliecerier.com/ [accessed in 2013].

Chamberlin, T.C., 1965, The Method of Multiple Working Hypotheses. *Science*, New Series, Vol. 148, No. 3671, pp. 754-759.

Champoux, P. W., 1999, *Gaia Matrix: Arkhom and the Geometries of Destiny in the North American Landscape*. Franklin Media, Washington, MA.

Chief Seattle, 1854, Chief Seattle's Message. In *Thinking Like a Mountain: Towards a Council of All Beings*, Seed, Macy, Fleming, Naess Eds., New Catalyst Books, Gabriola Island, BC, Canada.

Coleman, P.C., Bertuccio, L., Scarlett, Green Dove, Maggie, Donna, 2008, Simply Healthy: Creating Sustainable Communities. 3rd Annual Simply Living Fair and Wellness Expo of the Indiana Holistic Health Network and Center for Sustainability. Program Guide.

Colum, P., 1930, *The Orpheus Myths of the World*. Illustrations by Boris Artzybasheff [1930, copyright not renewed].

Connecting with the Land, 2013, Facebook page, URL: https://www.facebook.com/ConnectingWithTheLand/ [accessed on 6/21/2023].

Cooper, G., 1993, North America. In *Mythology: An illustrated guide*. Roy Willis Ed., Duncan Baird Publishers, London, UK.

Cornett, L., 1988, Nature Spirit Magic. URL: http://www.lcorncalen.com/NATURESPIRIT.htm [accessed in 2013].

Corrigan, I., 2000, *Druidheachd: Symbols and Rites of Druidry*. Starwood 2003 Edition.

Crossley-Holland, 1980, *The Norse Myths*. Random House, Inc., New York, NY.

Crowley, A., 1977, *777 and Other Qabalistic Writings of Aleister Crowley*. Edited and with an Introduction by Israel Regardie, Samuel Weiser, Inc., York Beach, ME.

Cunningham, S., 1988, *Cunninghmam's Encyclopedia of Crystal, Gem, & Metal Magic*. Llewellyn Publications, St. Paul, MN.

Cunningham, W.P., Cunningham, M.A., 2010, *Environmental Science: A Global Concern*, 11/e. McGraw Hill Education, Columbus, OH.

Davidson, H.E., 1993, Northern Europe. In *Mythology: An illustrated guide*. Roy Willis Ed., Duncan Baird Publishers, London, UK.

Davis, A.M., 2013a, Earth Science Principles and Exercises. URL: http://www.landsolution.com/teaching_resources.html [accessed on 6/19/2023].

Davis, A.M., 2013b, Photographs and Interpretations of Natural Features from Across North America. URL: http://www.landsolution.com/naturalfeatures.html [accessed on 6/19/2023].

Davis, A.M., 2013c, Environmental Links. URL: http://www.landsolution.com/envirolinks.html [accesssed in 2022].

Davis, A.M., 2011, Geoecology of abandoned agricultural fields in south central Indiana. Indiana University, 229 pages; URL: http://disexpress.umi.com/dxweb, UMI pub. number 3488051 [accessed in 2022].

Davis, A.M., 2004, Connecting with the Land: A primer.

Davis, A.M., 2002, Poem in: Connecting with Environments: Druids experience two forested hillside environments by Dobhran, Explore, Francesca, Skip, and White Owl, edited by Explore. *Oak Leaves*. The Quarterly Journal of Ár nDraíocht Féin. Issue No. 18.

Davis, A.M., 1999, In Connecting with the Land: A primer, Adam Davis Ed., 2004.

Defender's of Wildlife, 2013, http://www.defenders.org/ [accessed on 6/19/2023].

de Lint, C., 1998. *Greenmantle*. Orb Books, MacMillan Publishers, New York, NY.

Descartes, R., 2013, Reality is Beyond our Perception. CSGLOBE.

Dobhran, Explore, Francesca, Skip, and White Owl, 2002, Connecting with Environments: Druids experience two forested hillside environments. *Oak Leaves*. The Quarterly Journal of Ár nDraíocht Féin. Issue No. 18.

Doran, S., 2009. Personal communication.

Dr. Seuss, 1971, *The Lorax*. Random House, New York, NY.

Duquette, L.M., 1999, *My life with the spirits: The adventures of a modern magician*. Red Wheel/Weiser, LLC, York Beach, ME.

EarthSpirit, 2011, Rites of Spring 33 Program Guide.

Ellison, R.L., 2007, *Ogham: The Secret Language of the Druids*. Ár nDraíocht Féin Publishing, Tuscon, AZ.

Ellison, R.L., 2002, *The Druids Alphabet: What Do We Know About The Oghams*. Dragon's Keep Publishing, East Syracuse, NY.

Ellison, R.L., 2003, Getting in Touch with Your Land. Workshop.

Ellison, R.L., circa 2003, Tree workshop. Prince William Forest Park, VA.

Elsbeth, M., 1998, *Crystal Medicine*. Llewellyn Publications, St. Paul, MN.

EPA, 2013, Ecoregion Maps and GIS Resources. Environmental Protection Agency. URL: https//www.epa.gov/eco-research/ecoregions [accessed on 6/19/2023].

Evans, J., Perlman, H., 2013. The Water Cycle. Digital image. U.S. Geological Survey.

Ferguson, A.L.L., 1941, The Susquehannock Fort on Piscataway Creek. *Maryland Historical Magazine*, Vol. 36.

Fields, T.R., 2009, Kumu Pohaku (Stones as Teachers): Awakening to the Spiritual Dimension of Ecosystems. In *So What? Now What? The Anthropology of Consciousness Responds to a World In Crisis*, Matthew C. Bronson and Tina R. Fields Eds., UK: Cambridge Scholars Press, 2009 (pp. 317 – 359)., and Online at URL: http://indigenize.wordpress.com/about/spiritual-ecopsychology/kumu-pohaku-stones-as-teachers/ [accessed in 2013].

Fleming, P., Macy, J., 1988, The Council of All Beings. In *Thinking Like a Mountain: Towards a Council of All Beings*. Seed, Macy, Fleming, Naess Eds., New Catalyst Books, Gabriola Island, BC, Canada.

Forest Service, 2013, Legend of Seneca Rocks: The Betrothal of Snow Bird, Princess of the Seneca Indians. USDA Forest Service. Monongahela National Forest. Online [accessed in 2013].

Foundation For Deep Ecology, 2012, The Selected Works of Arne Naess. Web page summary, URL: http://www.deepecology.org/publishing_arne.htm [accessed in 2013].

Frost, R., 1923, "Stopping by Woods on a Snowy Evening" in *The Poetry of Robert Frost,* edited by Edward Connery Lathem. Copyright 1923, Copyright 1969 by Henry Holt and Company, Inc., renewed 1951, by Robert Frost.

Genesis 6-8, The Flood of Noah. *The Holy Bible*.

Gibran, K., 1927, *Sand and Foam*. Knopf Inc., New York, NY.

Global Footprint Network, 2023, URL: www.footprintcalculator.org [accessed on 3/21/2023].

Goddesses, 2010, Eagle Woman. *Maya del Mar's Daykeeper Journal*, URL: https://daykeeperjournal.com/2020/11/eagle-woman/ [accessed in 2010].

Goldhill, S., 1993, Greece: Goddesses of the Soil. In *Mythology: An illustrated guide*. Roy Willis Ed., Duncan Baird Publishers, London, UK.

Gore, A., 2000, *Earth in the Balance: Ecology and the Human Spirit*. Houghton Mifflin Company, New York, NY.

Gore, B., 1995, *Ecstatic Body Postures: An Alternate Reality Workbook*. Bear & Company Publishing, Santa Fe, NM.

Green Scissors, 2012, URL: http://greenscissors.com/ [accessed on 6/19/2023].

Greenwire, 2013, URL: http://www.eenews.net/gw [accessed on 6/19/2023].

Hahn, K., 2013, What is a food shed?. Michigan State University Extension, URL: http://msue.anr.msu.edu/news/what_is_a_food_shed/ [accessed in 2013].

Harner, M., 1990, *The Way of the Shaman*, Third Edition. HarperCollins Publishers, New York, NY.

Hill, M., 1984, *California Landscape: Origin and Evolution*. University of California Press, Berkeley, CA.

Hissom, P., 1999, Personal communication. Greenbelt Park, MD.

Hoffmann, D., 1996, *The Complete Illustrated Holistic Herbal: A Safe and Practical Guide to Making and Using Herbal Remedies*. Element Books Inc., Rockport, MA.

Hultkrantz, A., 1979, *The religions of the American Indians*. University of California Press, Berkeley, CA.

Indians.org, 2013, Cherokee Indian. URL: http://www.indians.org/articles/cherokee-indian.html [accessed in 2013].

IPCC, 2013, Intergovernmental Panel on Climate Change. URL: http://www.ipcc.ch/ [accessed on 6/19/2023].

Jack-in-the-Green Festival Committee, 2013, Hastings Traditional Jack-in-the-Green Festival. Online [accessed in 2013].

Jangl, A.M., and Jangl, J.F., 1985, *Ancient Legends of Gems and Jewels*. Prisma Press Publications, Coeur d'Alene, ID.

Johnsen, A., 2013, Product description of "The Goddess Pele" poster. Hawaii Parks online store. URL: https://shop.hawaiipacificparks.org/collections/art-prints-posters/products/pst-pele-aj-24x18 [accessed in 2013].

Jones, E., 2013, *Anemone lancifolia:* Mountain Anemone. In Wildflowers of Augusta County, VA.

Jones, G., Jones, T., 1993, *The Mabinogion*. Everyman's Library, Random House, New York, NY.

Jones, P., Pennick, N., 1995, *A History of Pagan Europe*. Barnes and Noble Books, New York, NY.

Kalavaris, K., 2013. Connecting with the land. Book Illustration.

Kozminsky, I., 1988, *The Magic and Science of Jewels and Stones, Vol. I*. Cassandra Press, San Rafael, CA.

Kunz, G.F., 1913, *The curious lore of precious stones*. J.B. Lippincott Company, Philadelphia, PA.

Lake-Thom, 1997, *Spirits of the Earth: A Guide to Native American Nature Symbols, Stories, and Ceremonies*. Plume, Penguin Books USA Inc., New York, NY.

Lane, P. (Philip Brown Bear), 2013, History of the Native American Flute. URL: http://www.wind-dancer-flutes.com/History_of_the_native_american_f.htm [accessed on 8/13/2023].

Lao Tzu, *Tao Te Ching*.

Lavine, T.Z., 1984, *From Socrates to Sartre: the Philosophic Quest*. Bantum Books, New York, NY.

Lawless, G., In *Earth Prayers From Around The World: 365 Prayers, Poems, and Invocations For Honoring The Earth*. Elizabeth Roberts and Elias Amidon Eds., 1991, HarperCollins Publishers, New York, NY.

League of Conservation Voters, 2013, http://www.lcv.org/ [accessed in 2013].

Leave No Trace, 2013, Leave No Trace: Center for Outdoor Ethics. Website URL: http://lnt.org/ [accessed in 2013].

Leopold, A., 1949, *A Sand County Almanac: With Other Essays on Conservation from Round River*. Oxford University Press, USA.

Levin, H., 2006, *The Earth Through Time*, Eighth Edition. John Wiley & Sons, Inc., Hoboken, NJ.

Livingstone, D. N., 1992, *The Geographical Tradition: Episodes in the History of a Contested Enterprise*. Blackwell Publishing, Oxford, UK.

Lockwood, J.P., Hazlett, R.W., 2010, Chapter 6. *Effusive Volcanic Eruptions and Their Products*. In *Volcanoes: Global Perspectives*. John Wiley & Sons, Hoboken, NJ.

Logan, K.N., 1997, *Clean House, Clean Planet: Clean Your House for Pennies a Day the Safe, Nontoxic Way*. Simon & Schuster, Inc., New York, NY.

London, 1908, To build a fire. *The Century Magazine*, v.76

Lovelock, J.E., 1979, *Gaia: A New Look at Life on Earth*. Oxford University Press, New York, NY.

Louv, R., 2012, Health benefits of being outdoors. *AARP Bulletin*, July 23, 2012 edition.

Luke, The Gospel according to Luke, In The Holy Bible.

MacCana, Proinsias, 1985, *Celtic Mythology*. New Revised Edition. Peter Bedrick Books, New York, NY.

Mac Coitir, N., 2003, *Irish Trees: myths, legends, and folklore*. The Collins Press, Ireland.

MacInnes, J., 1993, The Celtic World. In *Mythology: An illustrated guide*. Roy Willis Ed., Duncan Baird Publishers, London, UK.

McGAA, E., In *Earth Prayers From Around The World: 365 Prayers, Poems, and Invocations For Honoring The Earth*. Elizabeth Roberts and Elias Amidon Eds., 1991, HarperCollins Publishers, New York, NY.

McPhee, J., 1998, *Annals of the Former World*. Farrar, Straus, Giroux, New York, NY.

Manakee, H.R., 1959, *Indians of early Maryland*. Maryland Historical Society, Baltimore, MD.

Matthews, J., 2002, *The Green Man: Spirit of Nature*. Connections Book Publishing, London, UK.

Melody, 1995, *Love is in the Earth: A Kaleidoscope of Crystals: The Updated Reference Book Describing the Metaphysical Properties of the Mineral Kingdom*. Earth-Love Publishing House, Wheat Ridge, CO.

Miyazaki, H., 1997, Princess Mononoke. Written and directed by Hayao Miyazaki, animated by Studio Ghibli and produced by Toshio Suzuki.

Muir, J., 1912, The Yosemite. The Century Co., New York, NY.

Mythical Creatures List, 2013, Khyung. Online [accessed in 2013].

Mythology Dictionary, 2012, African Mythology. Online [accessed in 2012].

Nabhan, G.P., 2001, *Coming Home to Eat: The Pleasures and Politics of Local Foods*. W.W. Norton and Company.

Nathair Bheag, 1998, Ogham workshop.

Nees, J., 2004, Personal communication.

Neihardt, J.G., 1932, *Black Elk Speaks*. University of Nebraska Press, Lincoln, NE.

Newcomb, L., 1977, *Newcomb's Wildflower Guide: An Ingenious New Key System for Quick, Positive Field Identification of the Wildflowers, Flowering Shrubs, and Vines of Northeastern and North-central North America*. Little, Brown and Company, Boston, MA.

Paxson, D.L., 2005, *Taking up the runes: a complete guide to using runes in spells, rituals, divination, and magic*. Weiser Books, Boston, MA.

Peters, J., 2013, Jizo. In preparation.

Peterson, L.A., 1977, *A Field Guide to Edible Wild Plants: Eastern and Central North America*. Houghton Mifflin Company, Boston, MA.

Phillips, E., 2011, Descendants of Leonard Spaulding. Unpublished Geneology.

Pliny the Elder [Caius Plinius Secundus], 1956, *Natural History*. Harvard University Press, Cambridge, MA (Original work published 77-150 CE).

Porter, C.J.R., 1993, Middle East. In *Mythology: An illustrated guide*. Roy Willis Ed., Duncan Baird Publishers, London, UK.

Roberts, E., Amidon, E., 1991, *Earth Prayers from Around the World: 365 Prayers, Poems, and Invocations for Honoring the Earth*. HarperCollins Publishers, New York, NY.

Roberts, T.R., Roberts, M.J., Katz, B.P., 1997, *Mythology: Tales of Ancient Civilizations*. Barnes & Noble Books, New York, NY.

Rolleston, T.W., 1917, *Celtic Myths and Legends*. G.G. Harrap, London, UK.

Rosetree, R., 1996, *Aura Reading Through All Your Senses: Celestial Perception Made Practical*. Women's Intuition Worldwide, Sterling, VA.

Sakaki, N., In *Earth Prayers From Around The World: 365 Prayers, Poems, and Invocations For Honoring The Earth*. Elizabeth Roberts and Elias Amidon Eds., 1991, HarperCollins Publishers, New York, NY.

Seed, J., Macy, J., Fleming, P., Naess, A., 1988, *Thinking Like a Mountain: Towards a Council of All Beings*. New Catalyst Books, Gabriola Island, BC, Canada.

Sibley, J., 2009, Runes: Elder & Anglo-Saxon Futharks. Workshop. Rites of Spring.

Spiral Rhythm, 2001, Elemental Chant. Recorded musical piece on the "I Am ..." CD/album.

Spock, 1969, The Way To Eden, "Star Trek" TV series. Season 3, Episode 20, Written by Arthur Heinneman, Character played by actor Leonard Nemoy.

Steiger, B., 1997, *Totems: The Transformative Power of Your Personal Animal Totem*. HarperCollins, San Francisco, CA.

Stewart, R.J., 1990, *Celtic Gods, Celtic Goddesses*. Blandford, Cassell Wellington House, London, UK.

Stormdragon, 1998, Personal communication.

Stromberg, J., 2013, What is the Anthropocene and Are We in It? Efforts to label the human epoch have ignited a scientific debate between geologists and environmentalists. *Smithsonian* magazine. URL: http://www.smithsonianmag.com/science-nature/What-is-the-Anthropocene-and-Are-We-in-It-183828201.html [accessed in 2013].

Suzuki, S., 1970, *Zen Mind, Beginner's Mind: Informal talks on Zen meditation and practice*. Weatherhill, Inc., New York, NY.

Tacitus, circa 98 CE, *Germania*.

Tchaikovsky, A., 2010. Shadows of the Apt. Novel Series. Prometheus Books, Amherst, NY.

Thich Nhat Hanh, In *Earth Prayers From Around The World: 365 Prayers, Poems, and Invocations For Honoring The Earth*. Elizabeth Roberts and Elias Amidon Eds., 1991, HarperCollins Publishers, New York, NY.

Tolkien, J.R.R., 1954, *The Two Towers*. Second Volume of The Lord of the Rings. George Allen & Unwin, England.

USDA, 2013, USDA Plants Database. U.S. Department of Agriculture, URL: http://plants.usda.gov [accessed on 6/19/2023].

Vermont Wilderness School, 2007, Vermont Wilderness School Home Page. URL: http://vermontwildernessschool.org/school/ [accessed in 2013].

Voyageur Outward Bound School, 2013. Voyageur Outward Bound Homepage. URL: http://www.vobs.org [accessed in 2013].

Waterhawk, D., 2002, Tsalagi Dance of Life. Workshop. Sirius Rising. Sherman, NY.

Wessels, T., 2001, *The Granite Landscape: A Natural History of America's Mountain Domes, from Acadia to Yosemite*. The Countryman Press, Woodstock, VT.

Whitefeather, Bill, 2004, Sweat lodge ceremony and associated personal communication.

Whitman, W., In *Earth Prayers From Around The World: 365 Prayers, Poems, and Invocations For Honoring The Earth*. Elizabeth Roberts and Elias Amidon Eds., 1991, HarperCollins Publishers, New York, NY. Pg. 215.

Wikipedia, 2013a, Yunmen Wenyan. URL: http://en.wikipedia.org/wiki/Ummon [accessed in 2013].

Wikipedia, 2013b, Pliny the Elder. URL: http://en.wikipedia.org/wiki/Pliny_the_Elder [accessed in 2013].

Wikipedia, 2013c, The Gundestrup Cauldron. URL: http://en.wikipedia.org/wiki/Gundestrup_cauldron [accessed in 2013].

Wikipedia, 2013d, Nerthus. URL: http://en.wikipedia.org/wiki/Nerthus [accessed in 2013].

Wilderness Society. 2012, Radio Commercial. Broadcast 8/15/2012 15:47 EDT.

Wilkinson, P., Philip, N., 2007, *Mythology*. Visual Reference Guides. Metro Books, New York, NY.

Willis, R., 1993a, Africa. In *Mythology: An illustrated guide*. Roy Willis Ed., Duncan Baird Publishers, London, UK.

Willis, R., 1993b, Great Themes of Myth: Cosmic Architecture. In *Mythology: An illustrated guide*. Roy Willis Ed., Duncan Baird Publishers, London, UK.

Wojtech, M., 2011, *Bark: A Field Guide to Trees of the Northeast*. University Press of New England, Lebanon, NH.

Wolf Moondance, 2004, *Vision Quest: Native American Magical Healing*. Sterling Publishing Co., Inc., New York, NY.

Woods, B., 2001, Qi Gong. Workshop. Sirius Rising. Sherman, NY.

Wright, J., In *Earth Prayers From Around The World: 365 Prayers, Poems, and Invocations For Honoring The Earth*. Elizabeth Roberts and Elias Amidon Eds., 1991, HarperCollins Publishers, New York, NY.

Yatskievych, K., 2000, *Field Guide to Indiana Wildflowers*. Indiana University Press, Bloomington, IN.

Young, J., Haas, E., McGown, E., 2010, *Coyote's guide to connecting with nature*. Second Edition. Owlink Media Corporation, Shelton, WA.

Zalasiewicz, J., Williams, M., Smith, A., Barry, T.L., Coe, A.L., Bown, P.R., Brenchley, P., Cantrill, D., Gale, A., Gibbard, P., Gregory, F.J., Hounslow, M.W., Kerr, A.C., Pearson, P., Knox, R., Powell, J., Waters, C., Marshall, J., Oates, M., Rawson, P., Stone, P., 2008, Are we now living in the Anthropocene? *GSA Today*, v. 18, no. 2.

Zell, O., 1998, Millennial Gaia, Mother Earth. Statue.

ABOUT THE AUTHOR

Adam M. Davis is pledged in service to land and people. He is an experienced multidisciplinary naturalist and geologist, and he enjoys teaching about the Earth as a system of connected energy movements in classrooms and in the field. He also enjoys leading nature connection workshops at healthy living fairs, community events, and various other types of gatherings. He combines multiple perspectives and techniques to explore integrated, holistic ways of working with nature.

Adam is committed to helping diverse people learn about the Earth and connect with its energies. His 15 years of experience teaching earth and environmental science at the college level as well as over 25 years of experience leading spiritually oriented nature awareness exercises support him in providing customized experiences for individuals and groups. He has facilitated events of the Connecting with the Land Workshop Series at conferences and gatherings across North America. Connecting with the Land workshops create an intellectual and energetic environment that allows participants to enhance their awareness of sacred aspects of places and develop nature connections. Adam has also facilitated a variety of ceremonies, journeys, and meditation groups. His ritual and energy work skills come from many sources including training in the facilitation of multiple kinds of ceremonies, training in Reiki and Qi Gong, and a diverse personal spiritual practice.